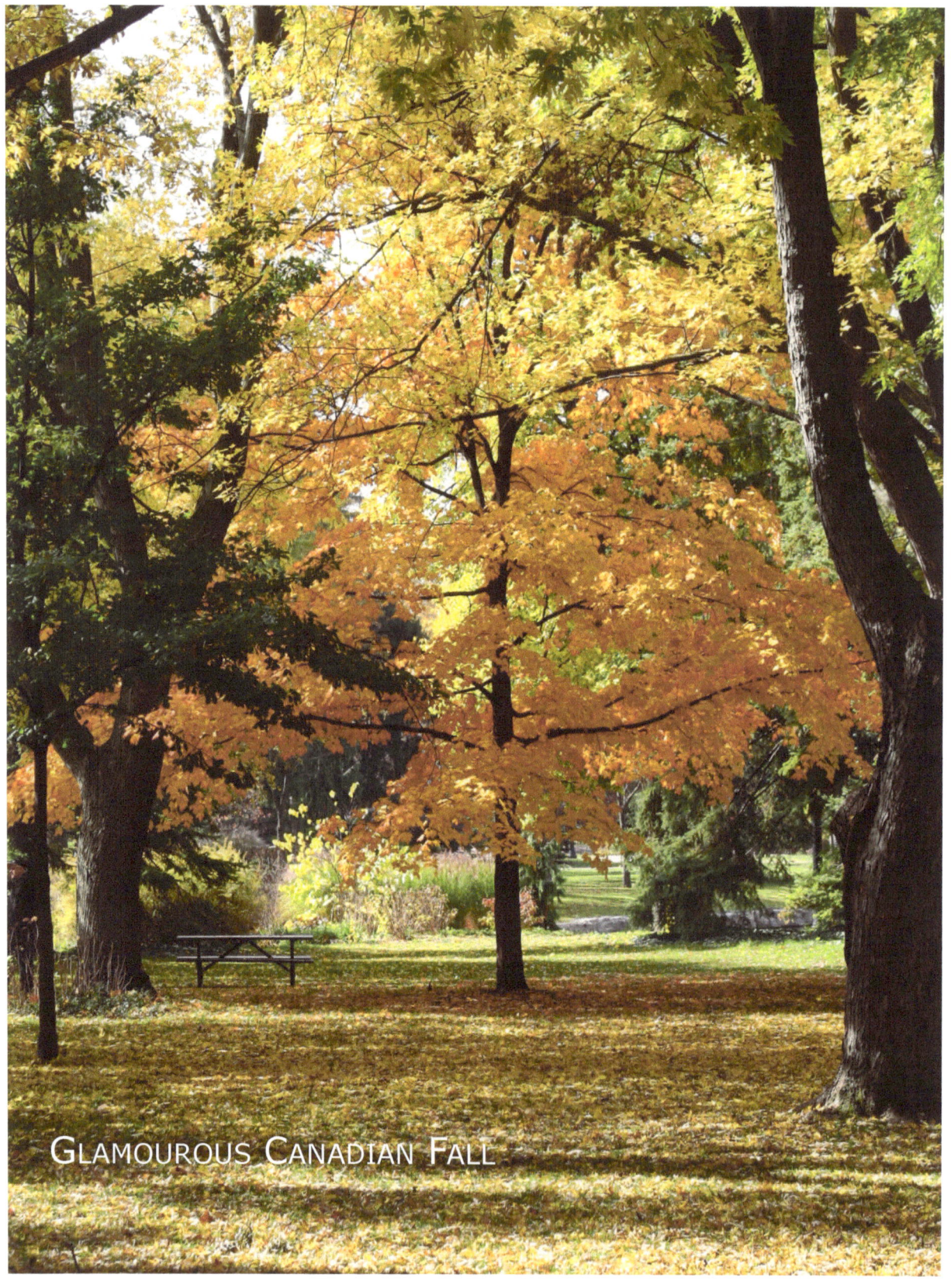

GLAMOUROUS CANADIAN FALL

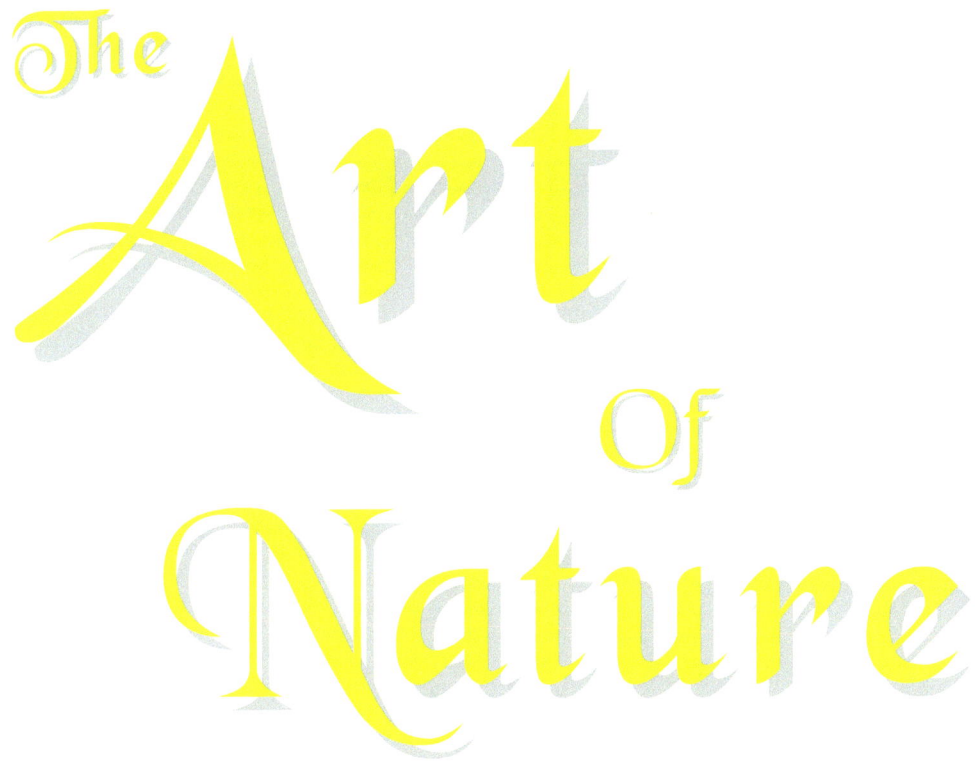

The Art Of Nature

PHOTOGRAPHY

KLAUS D. EMRICH

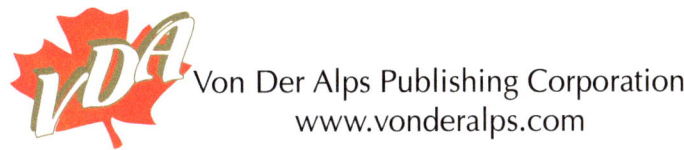

Von Der Alps Publishing Corporation
www.vonderalps.com

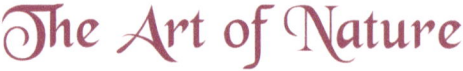

The Art of Nature

Author/Photographer

Klaus D. Emrich

First original published in April 2014 by
Von Der Alps Publishing Corporation, CANADA.

www.vonderalps.com

Canadian Cataloguing in Publication Data
ISBN 978-0-9782302-8-9

Printed in USA

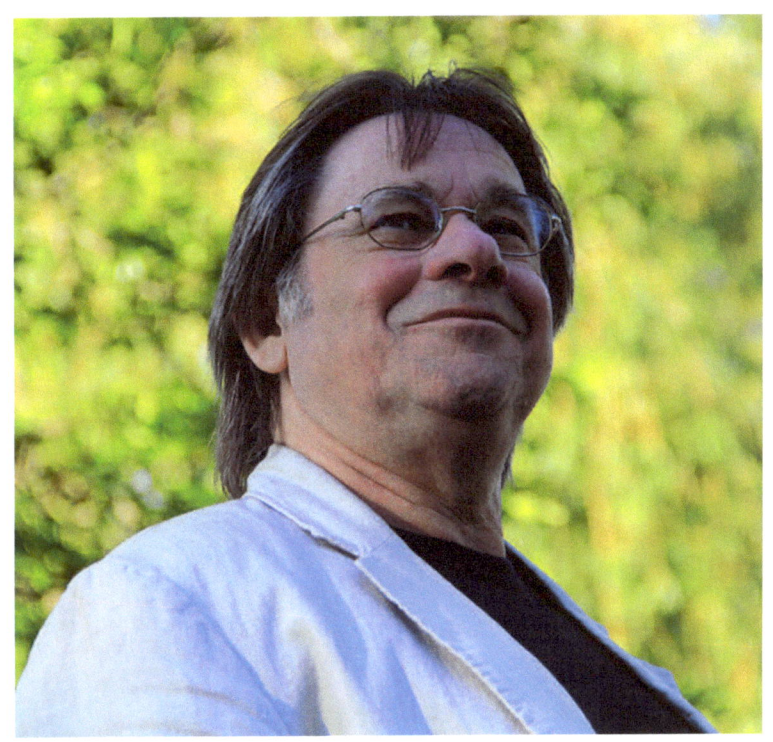

KLAUS D. EMRICH

THIS BOOK IS DEDICATED TO MY WIFE MARY EMRICH
(PEN NAME ELYSSE POETIS - AWARD WINNING AUTHOR/POET/PHOTOGRAPHER ON AMAZON).
DUE TO HER LOVE AND INSPIRATION THIS BOOK WAS POSSIBLE.

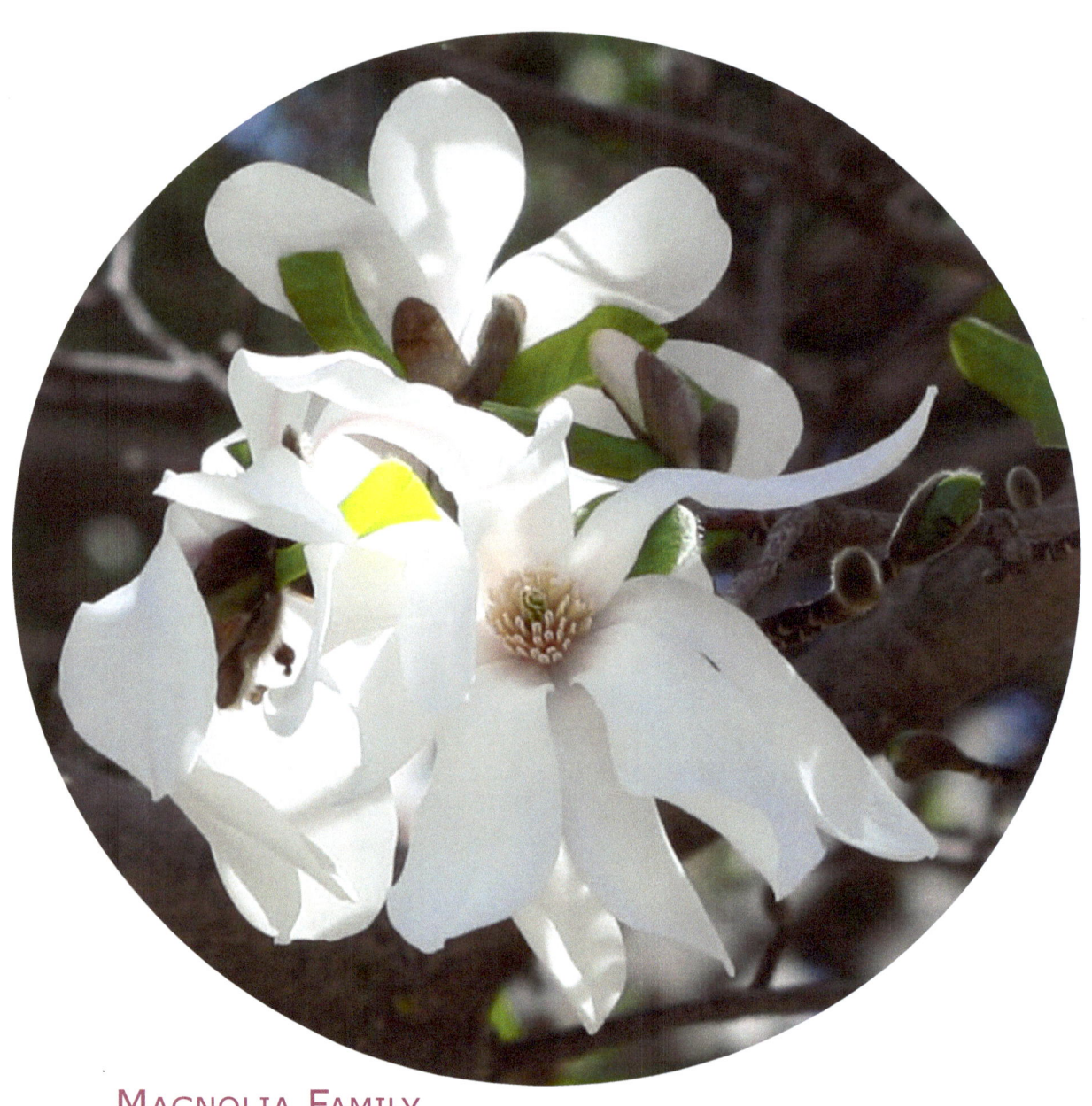

MAGNOLIA FAMILY

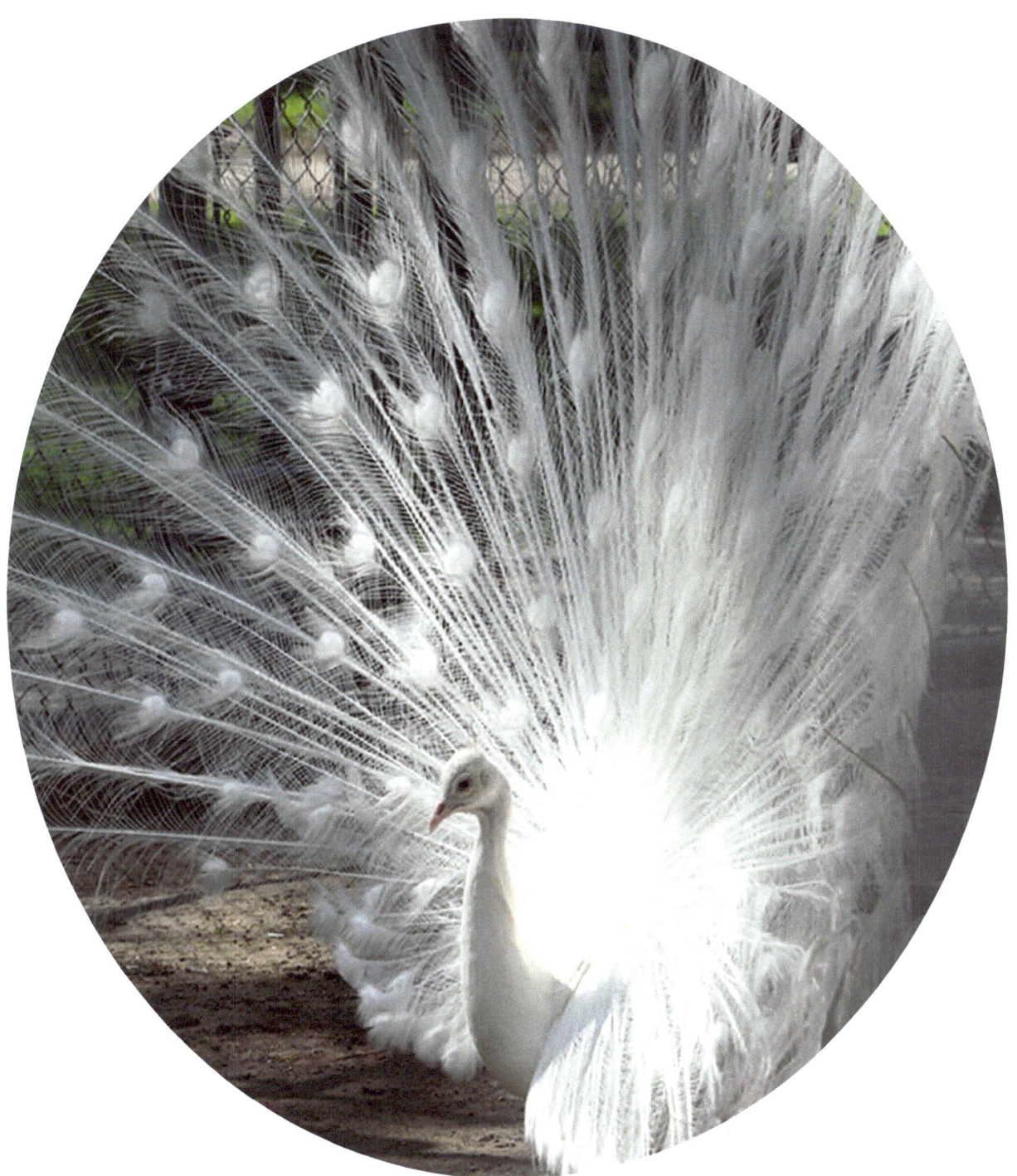

LOOKING FOR BEAUTY?
LOOK NO FURTHER

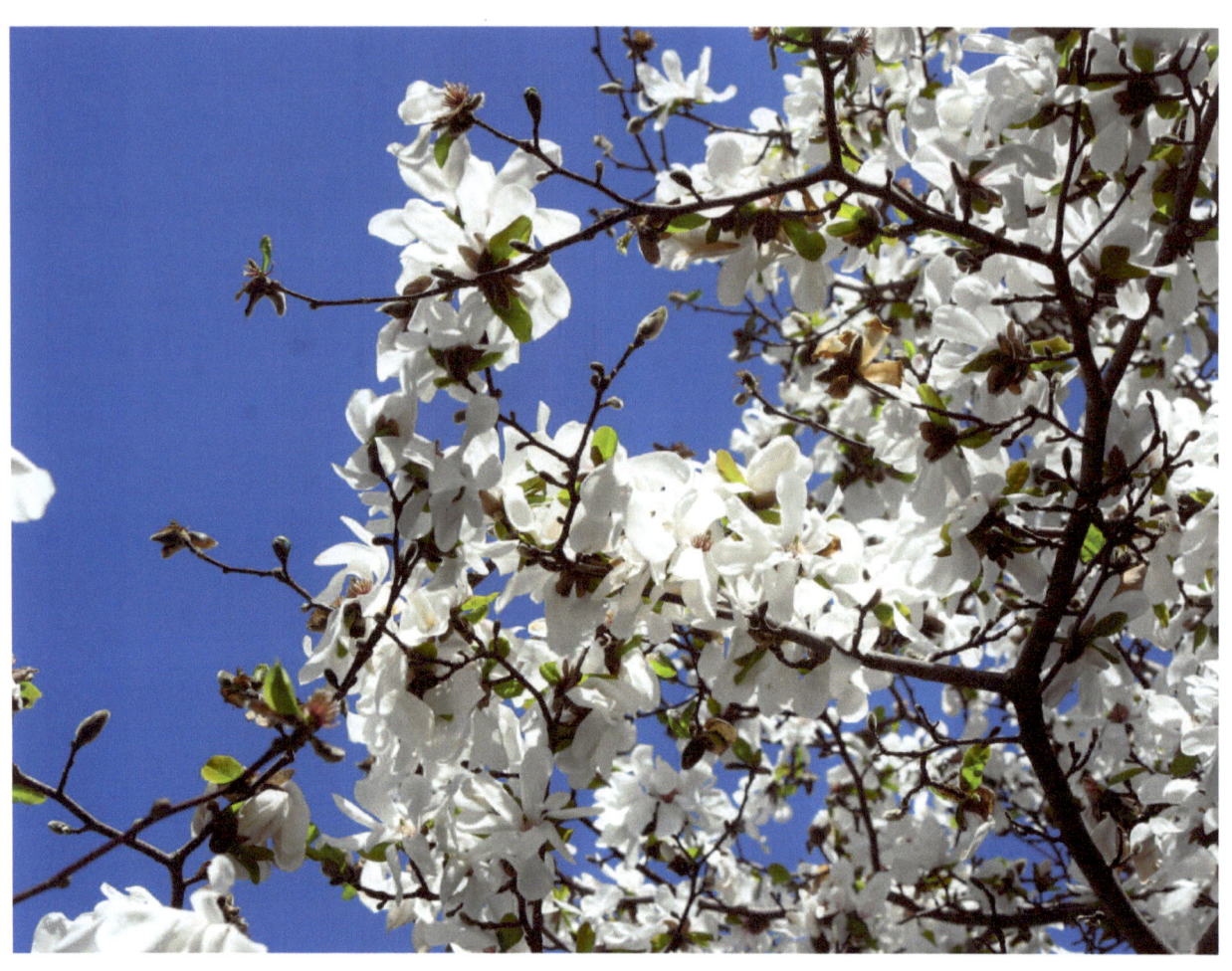

THE PEACE YOU FIND JUST BY
LOOKING AT A BLOSSOMED TREE

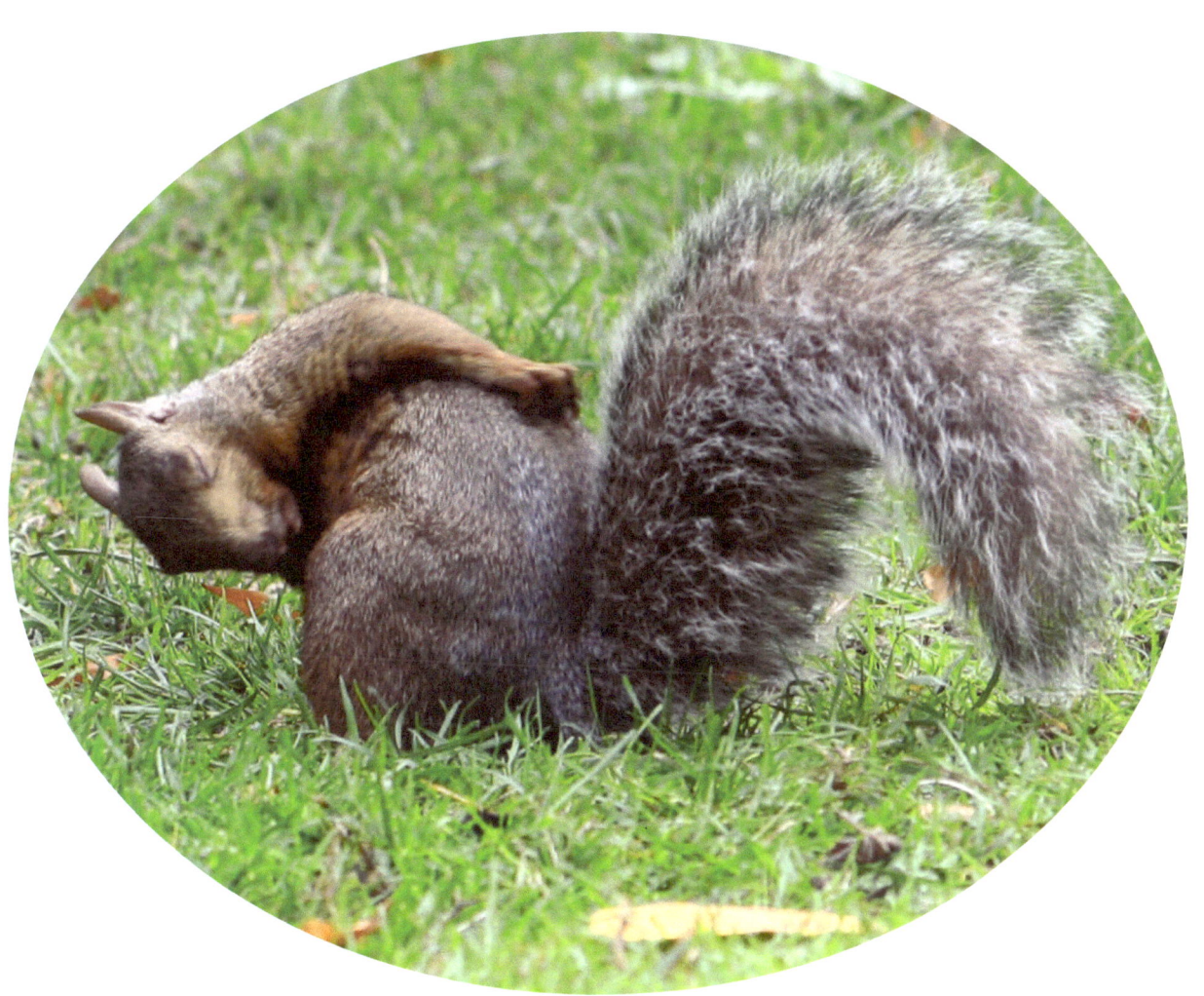

OH, THE ITCH I HAVE TODAY

I AM THE BIG FELLOW HERE

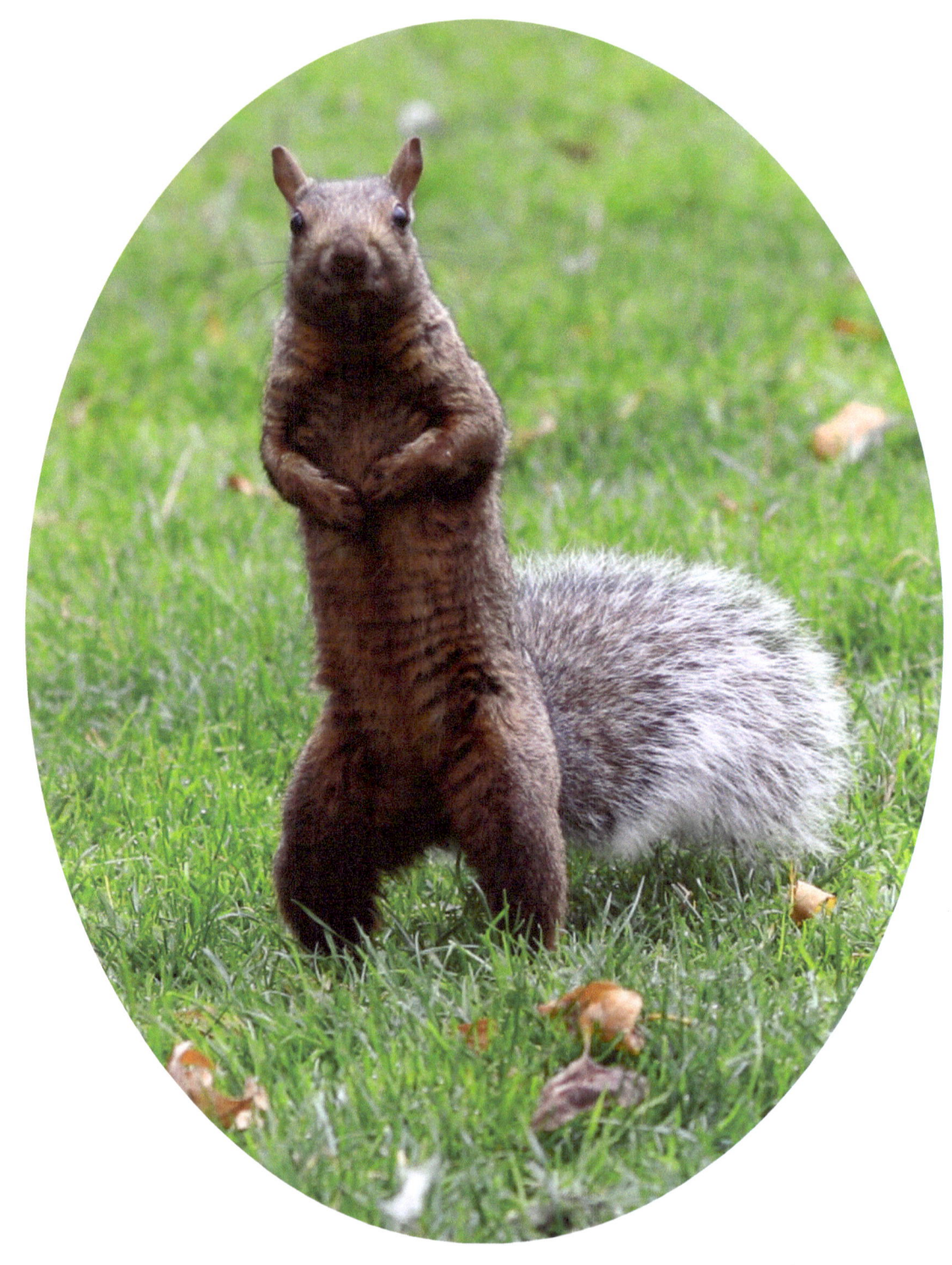

The Art of Nature

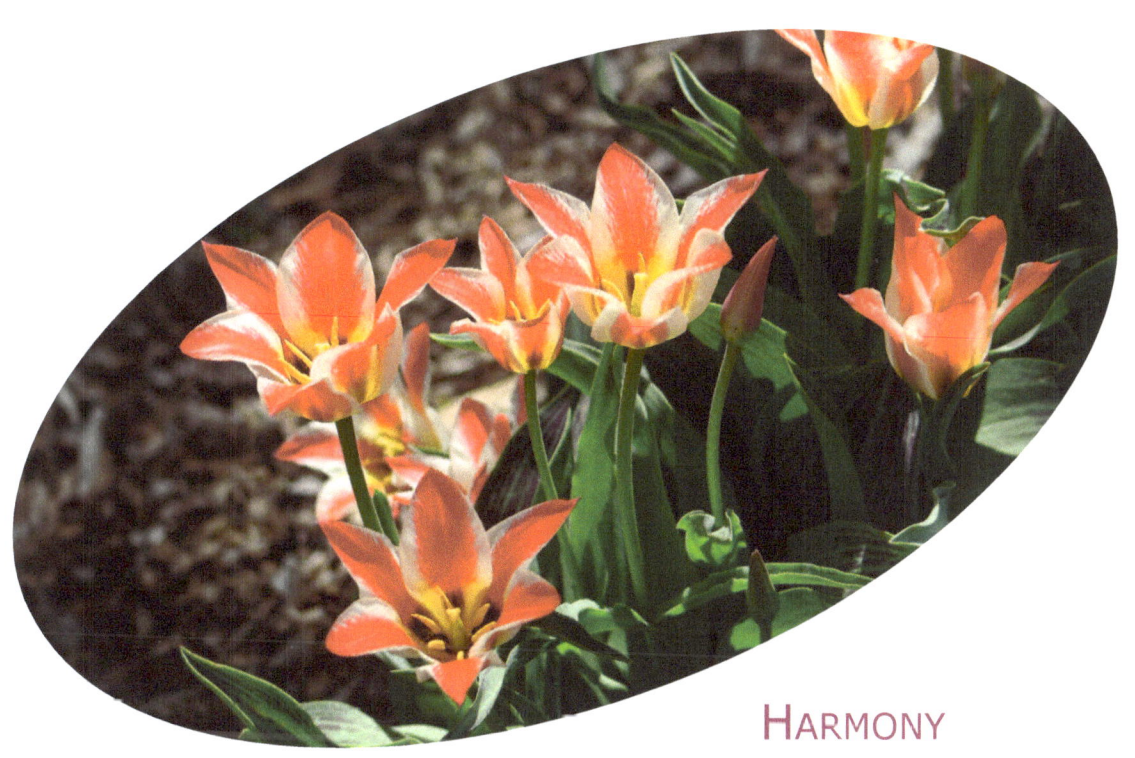

HARMONY

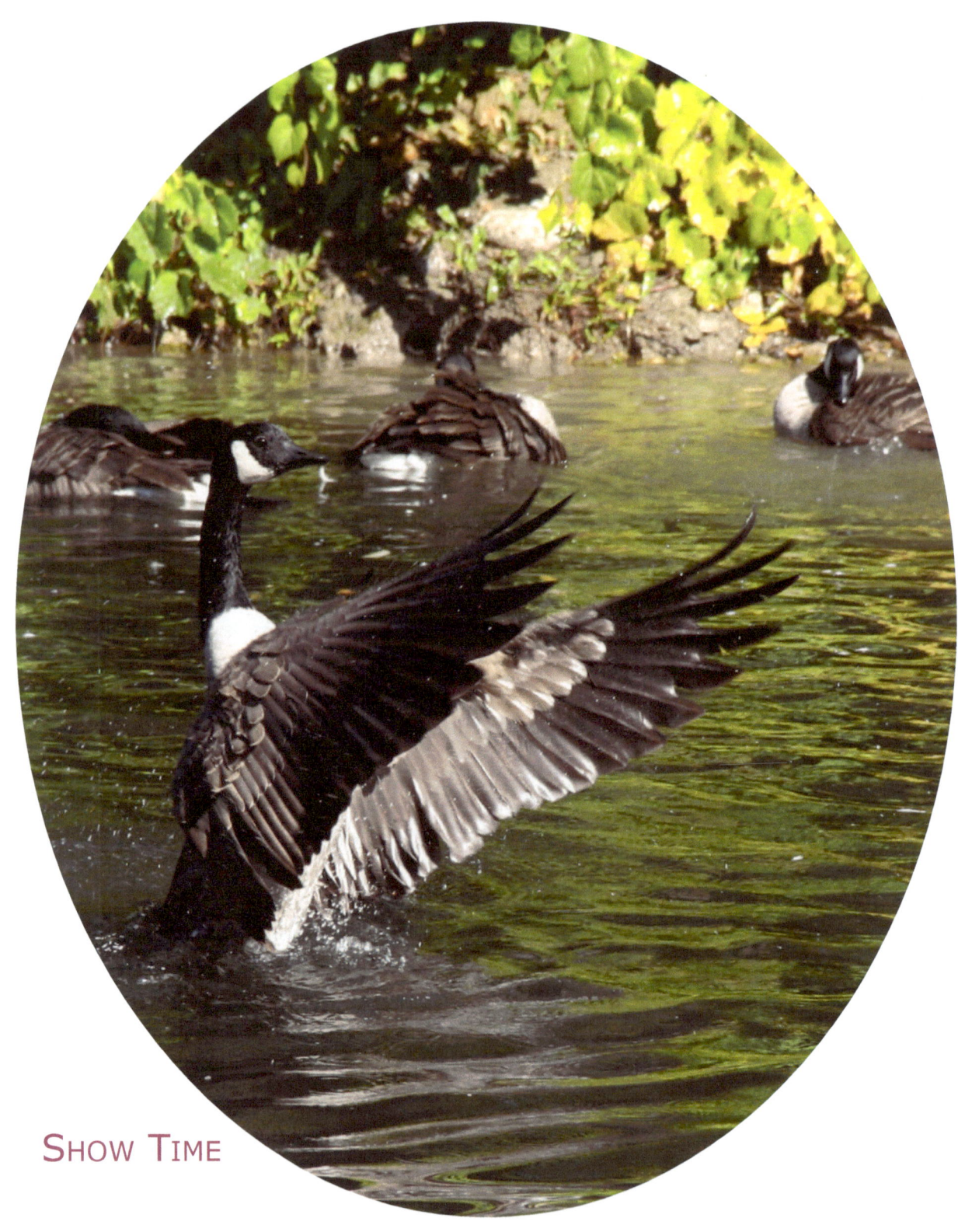

SHOW TIME

I AM LOOKING FOR A NEW
HOME

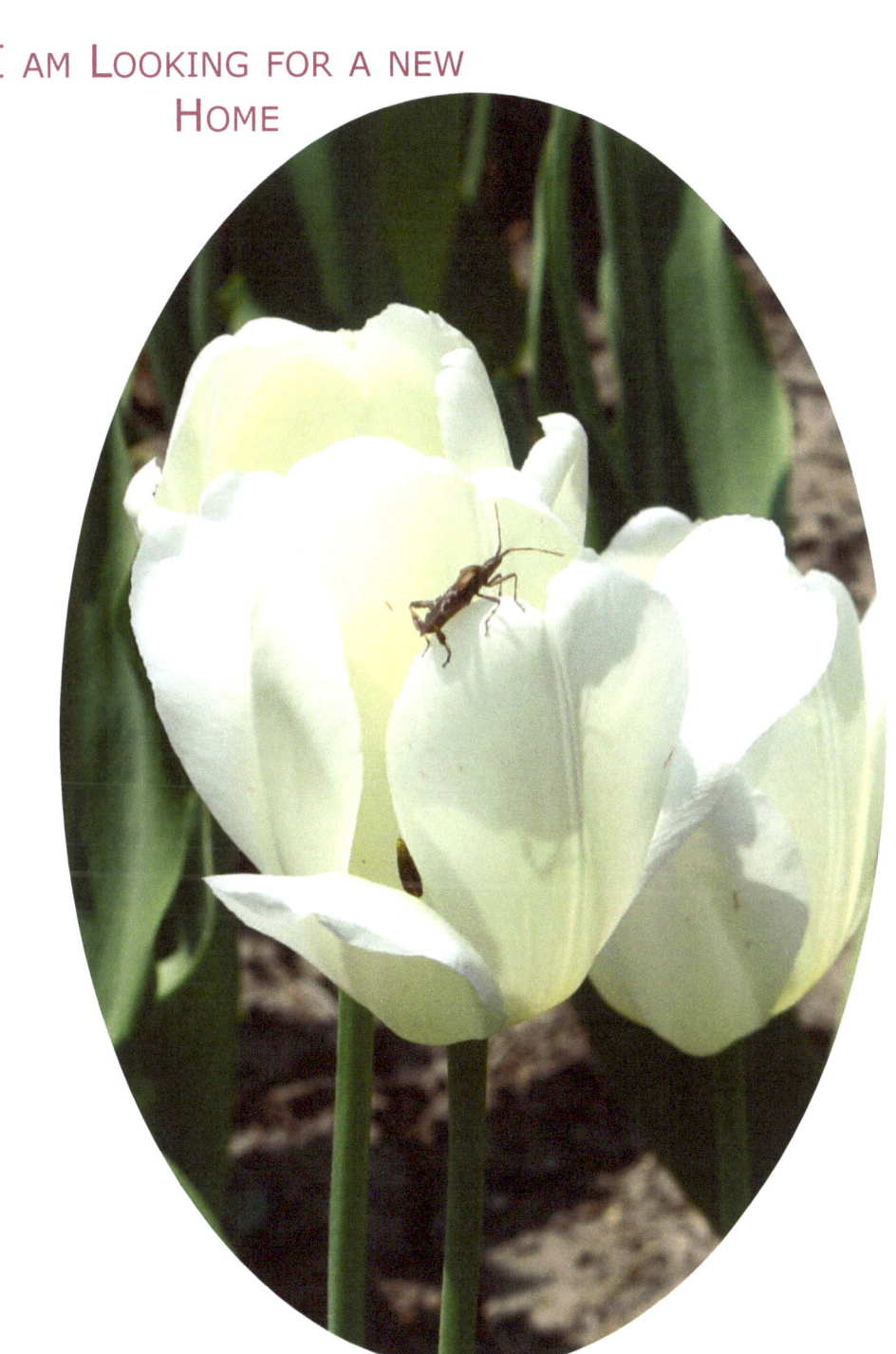

YELLOW MAGIC

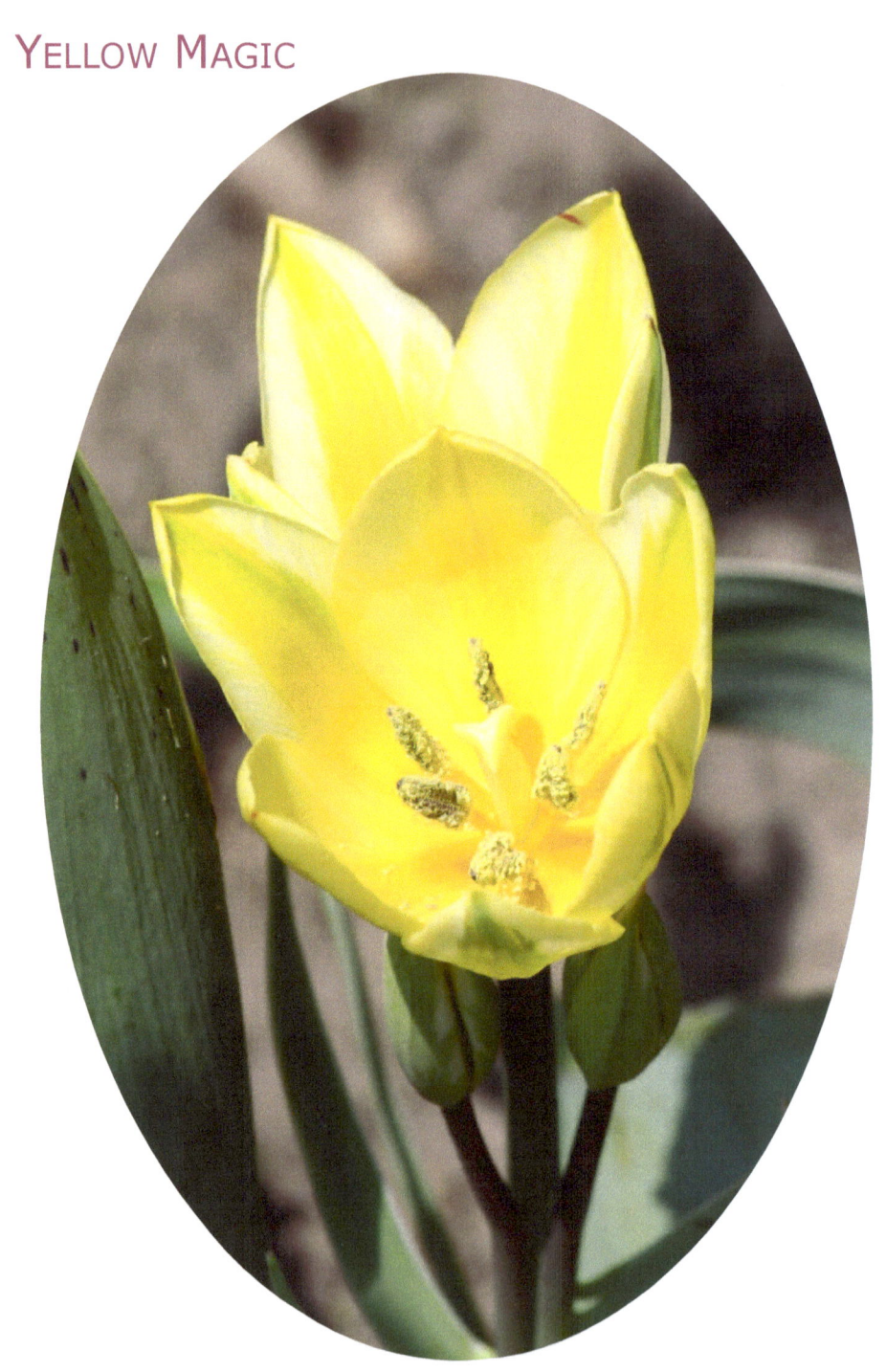

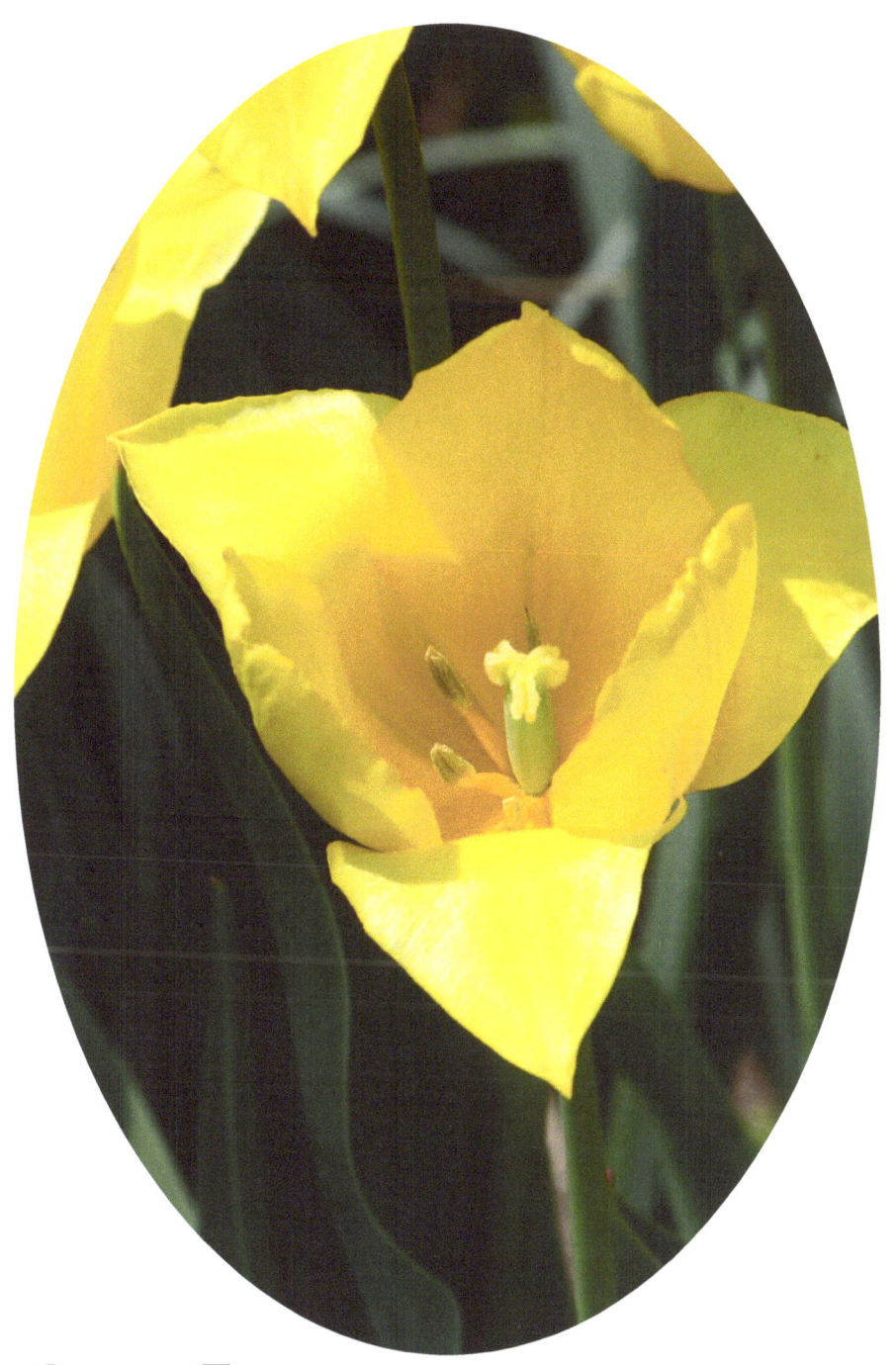

GOLDEN TREAT

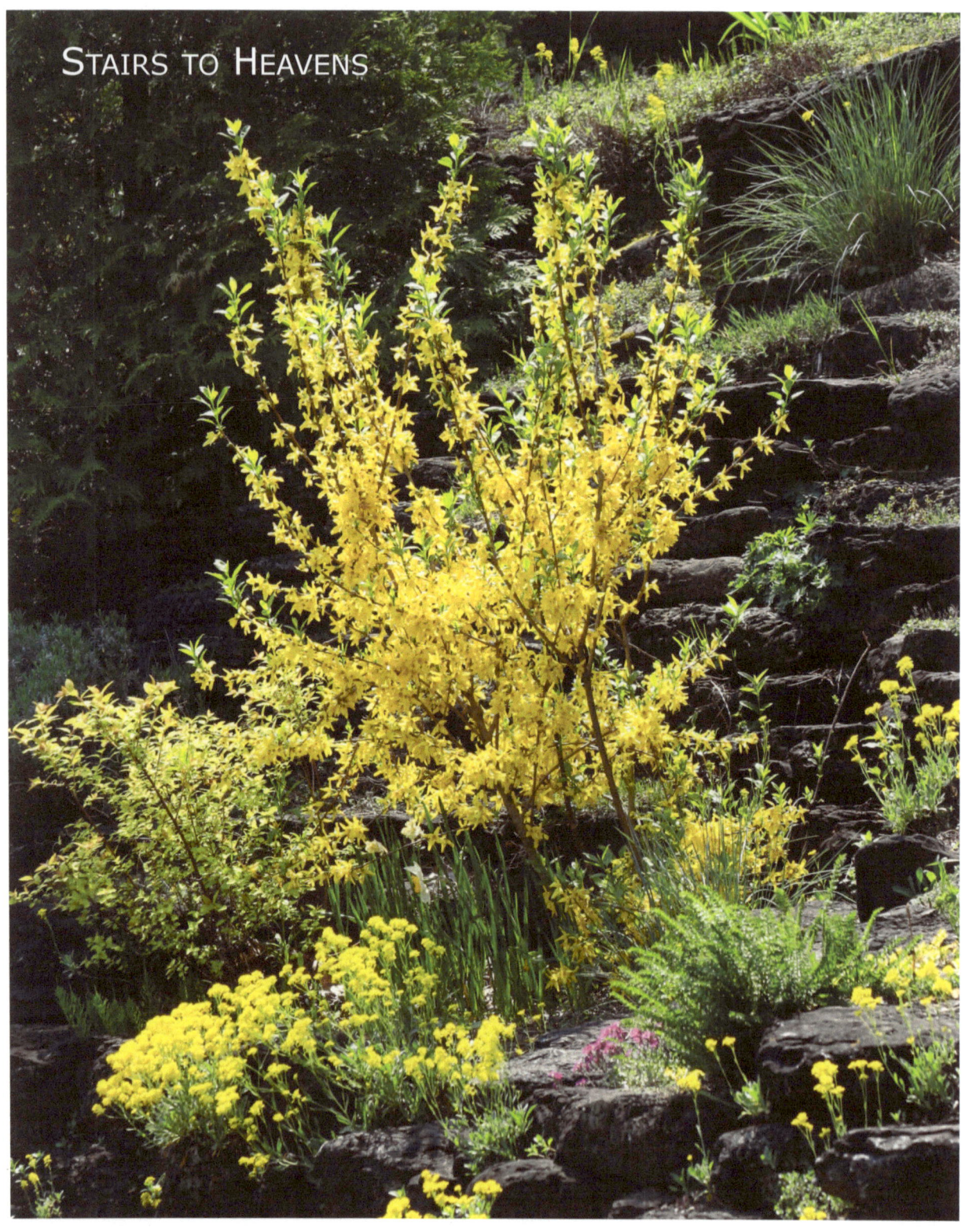

STAIRS TO HEAVENS

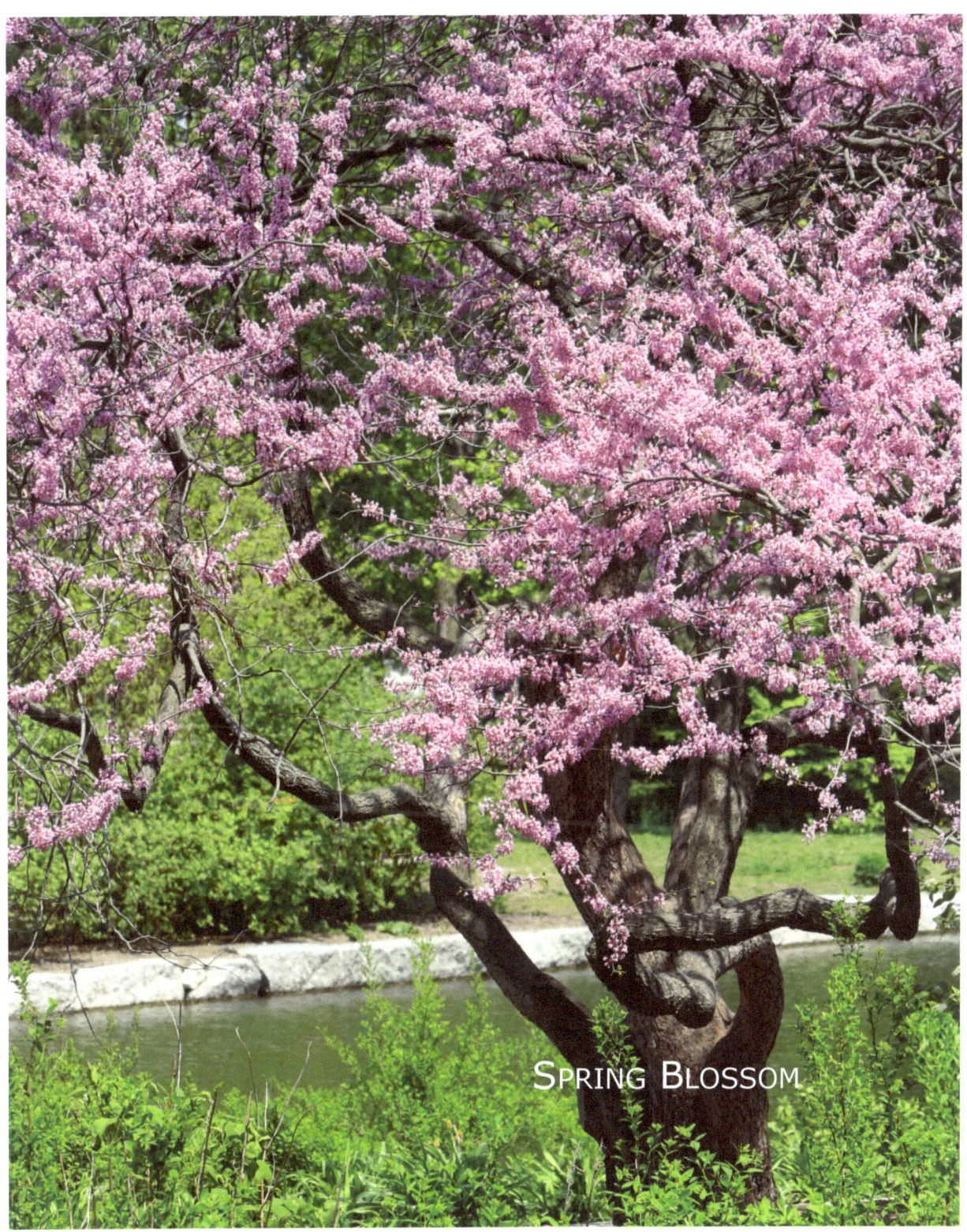

SPRING BLOSSOM

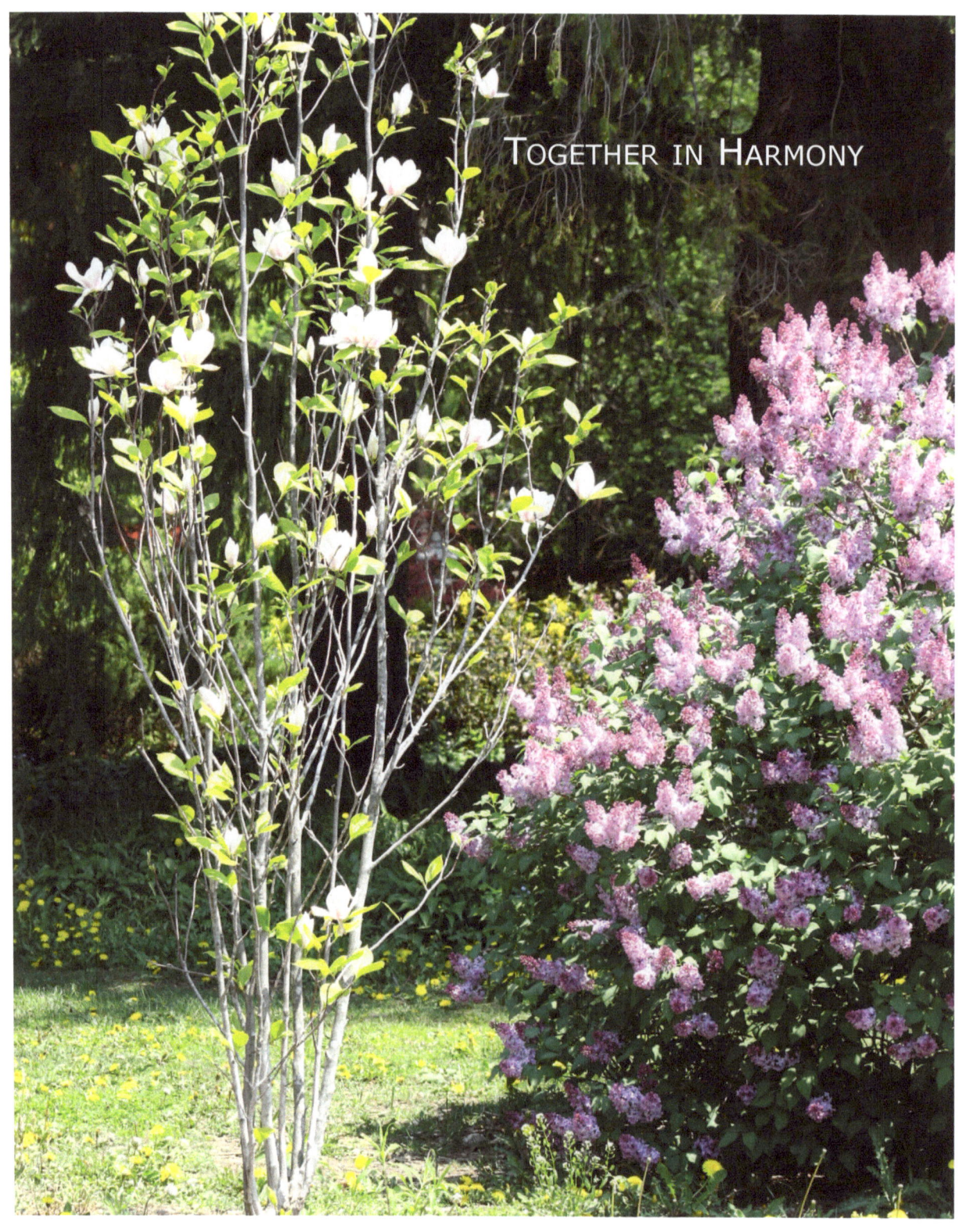

TOGETHER IN HARMONY

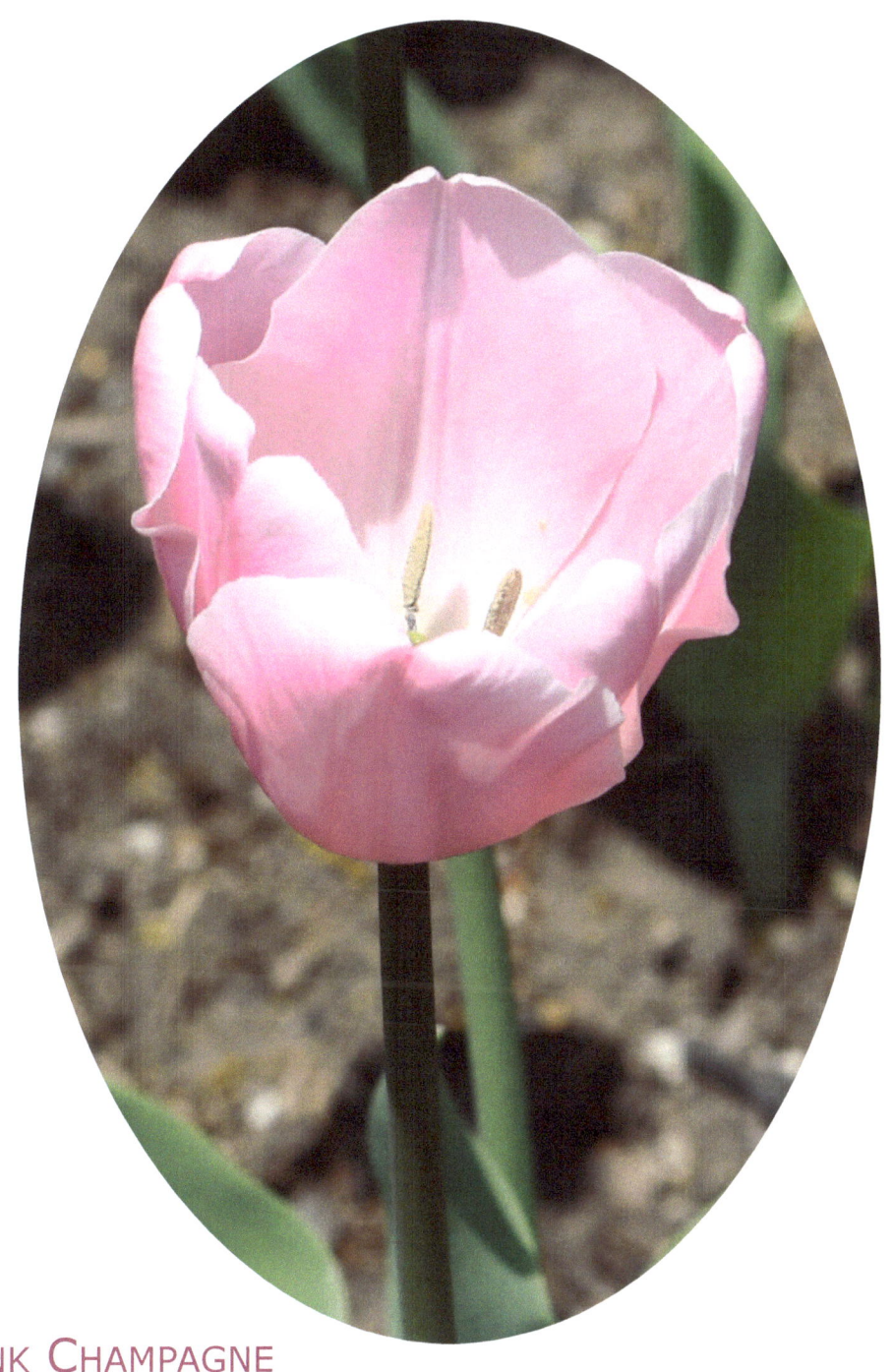

PINK CHAMPAGNE

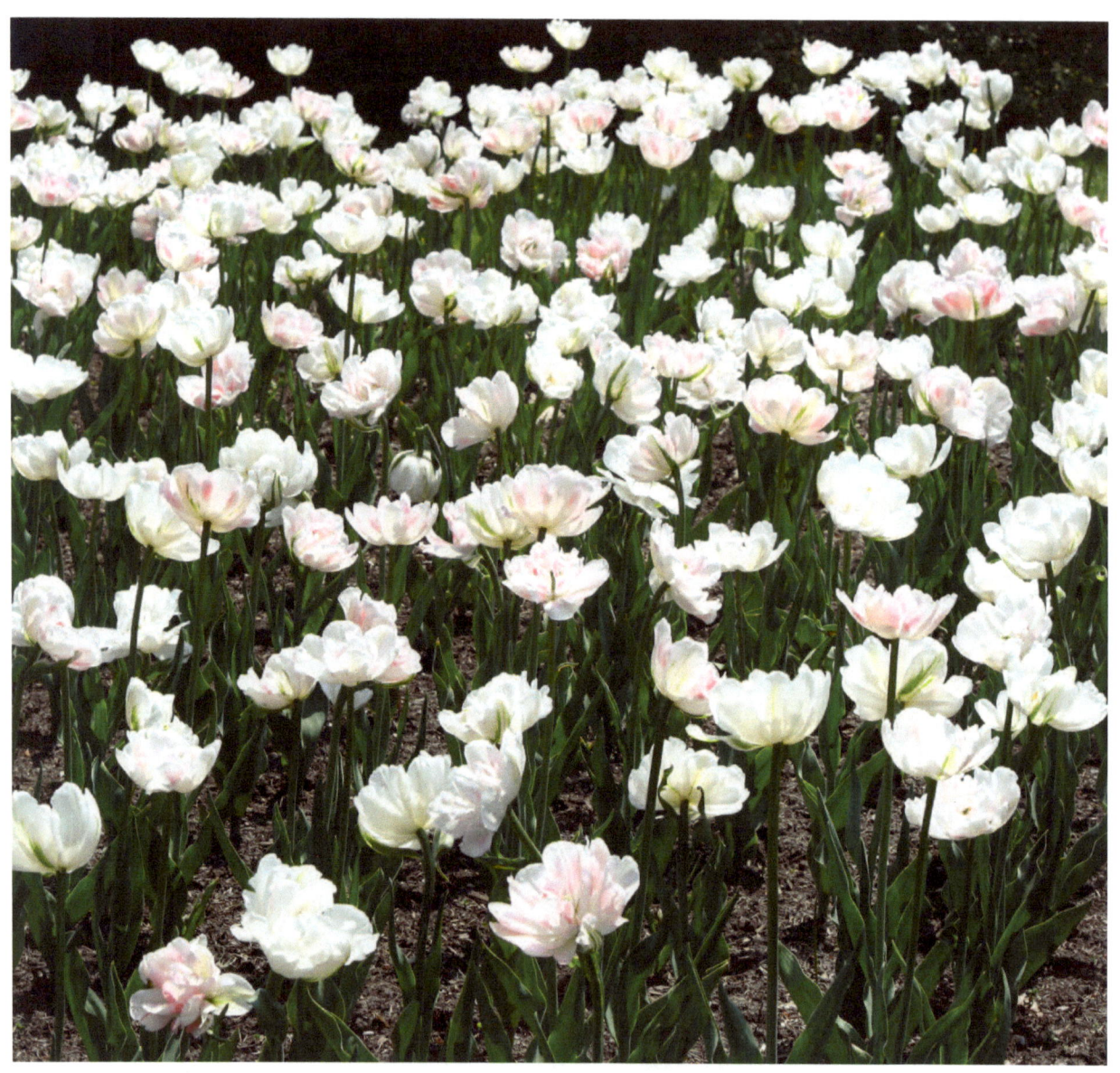

FIELD OF DREAMS

I AM THE
FRONTRUNNER

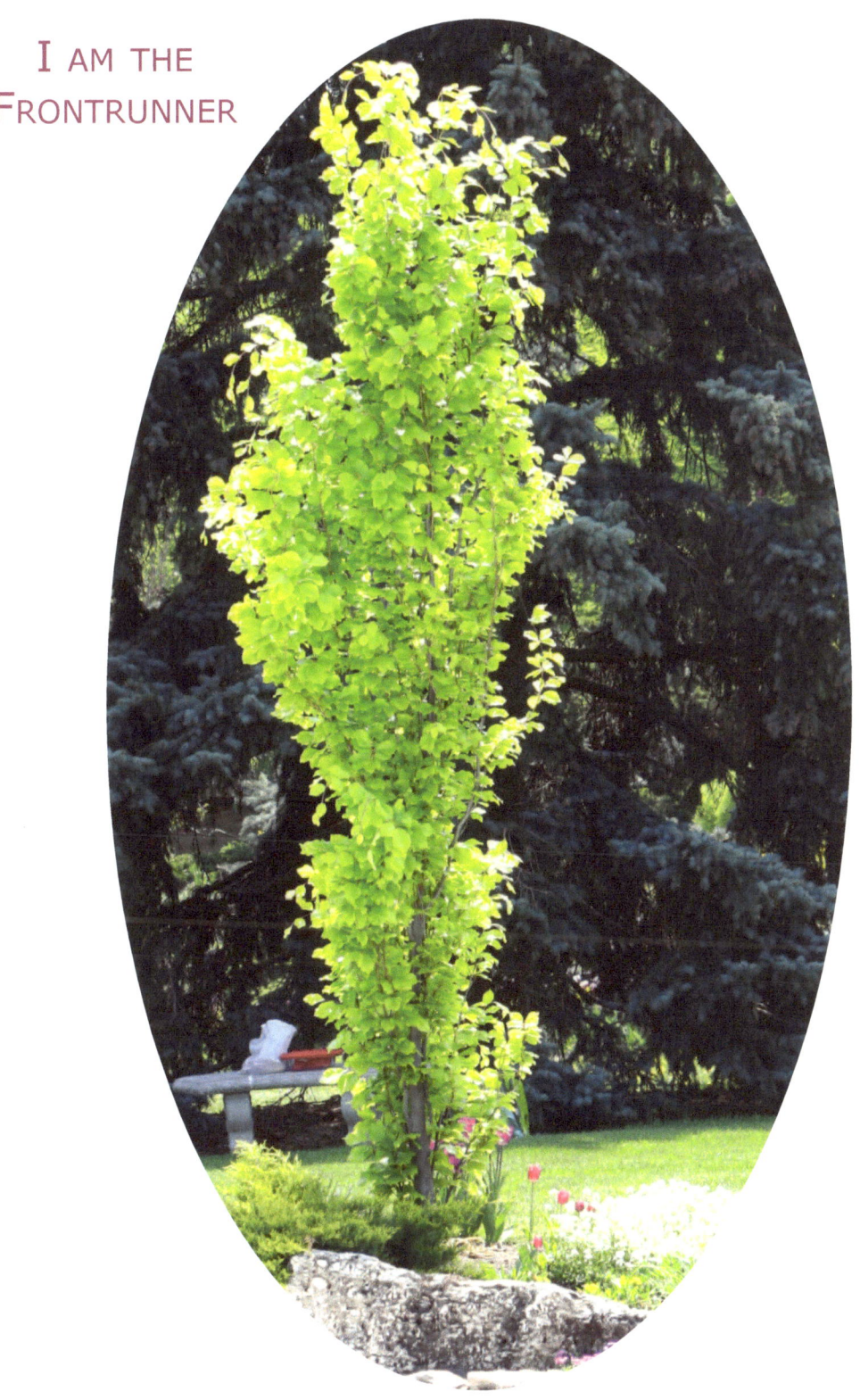

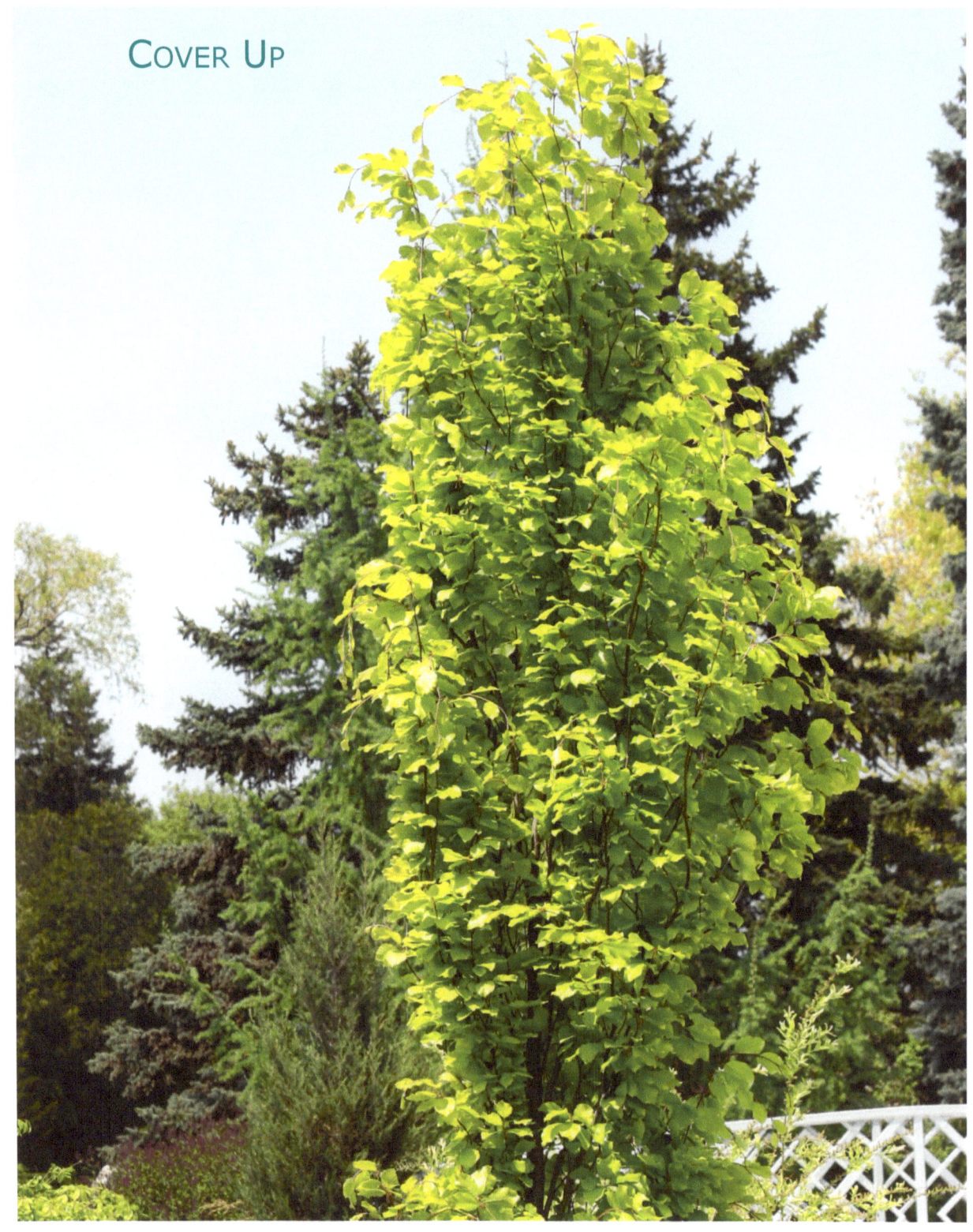

COVER UP

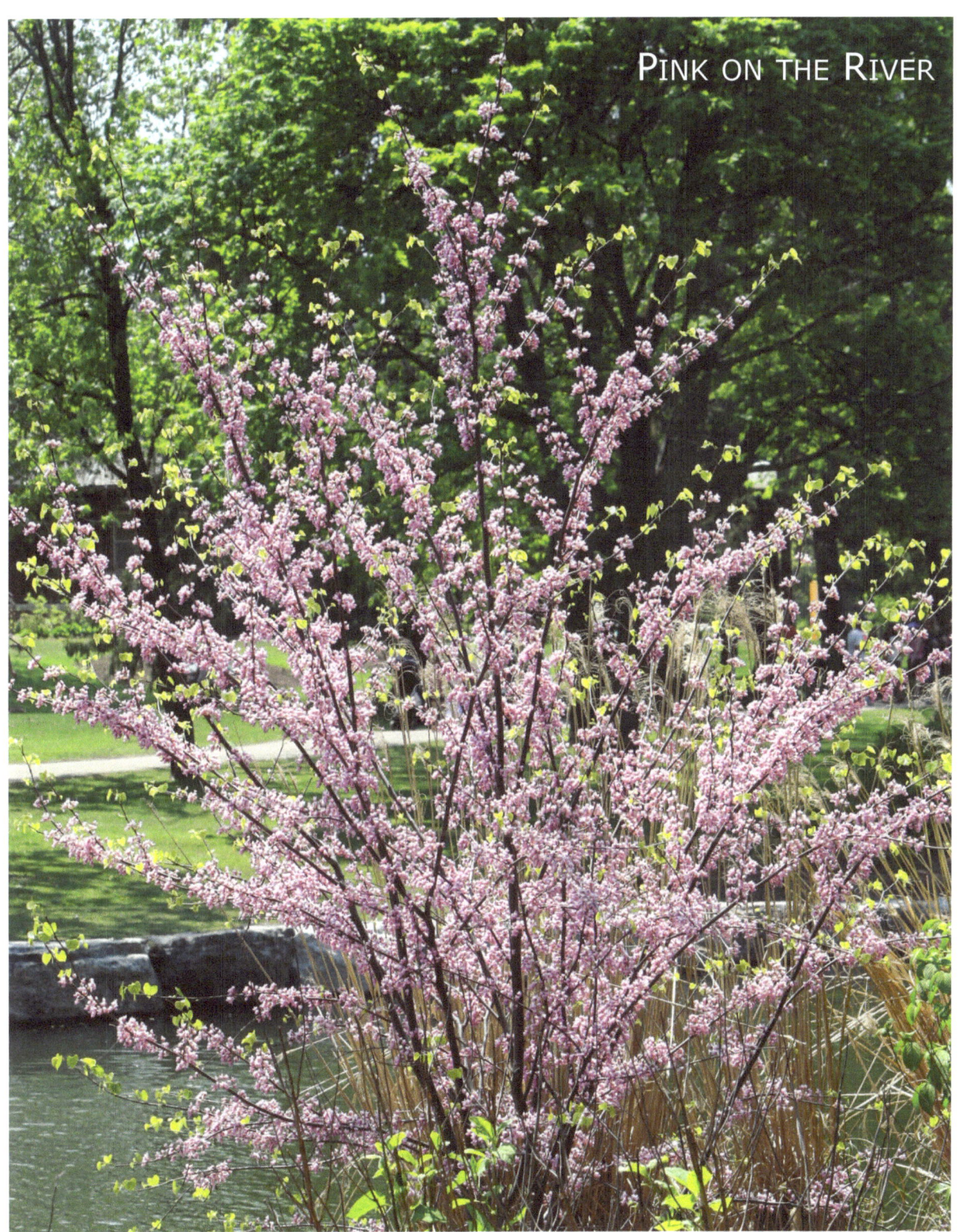

PINK ON THE RIVER

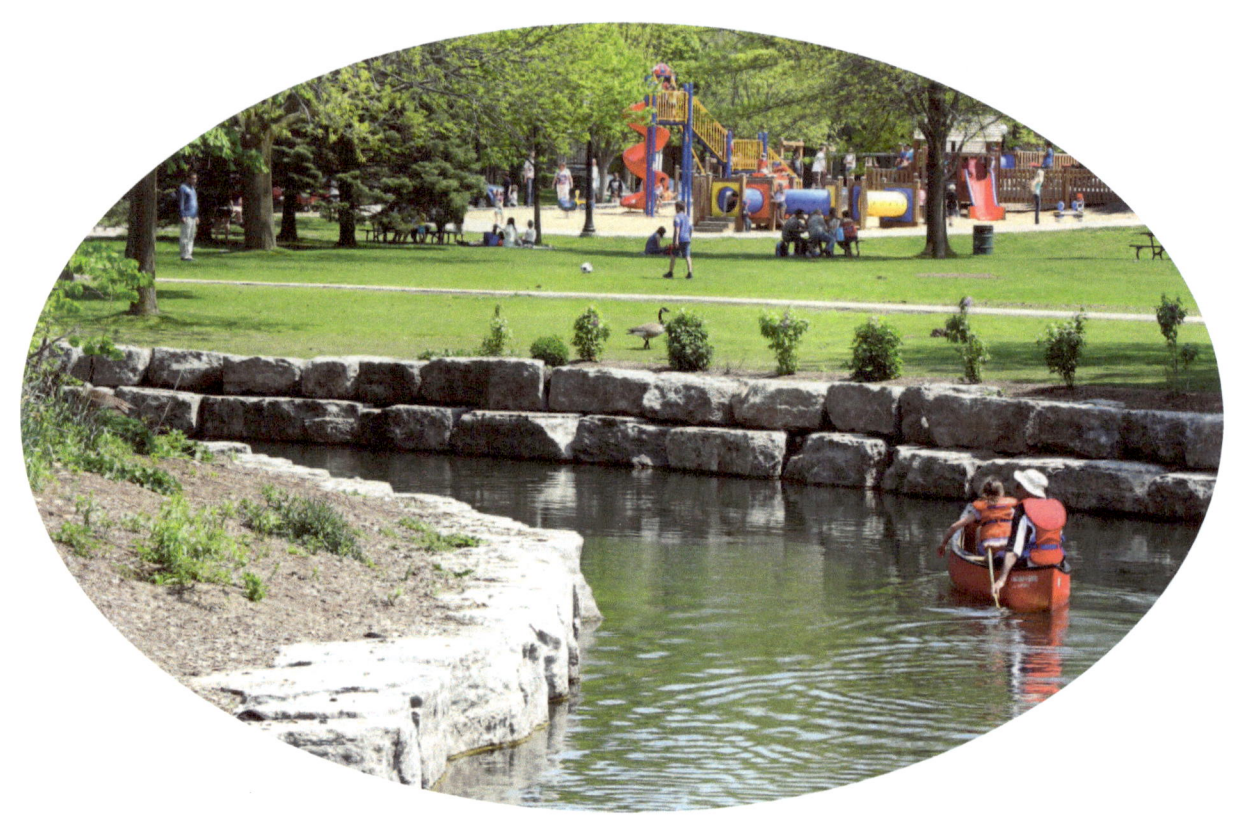

FAMILY FUN IN THE PARK

Look! I can flap my Wings

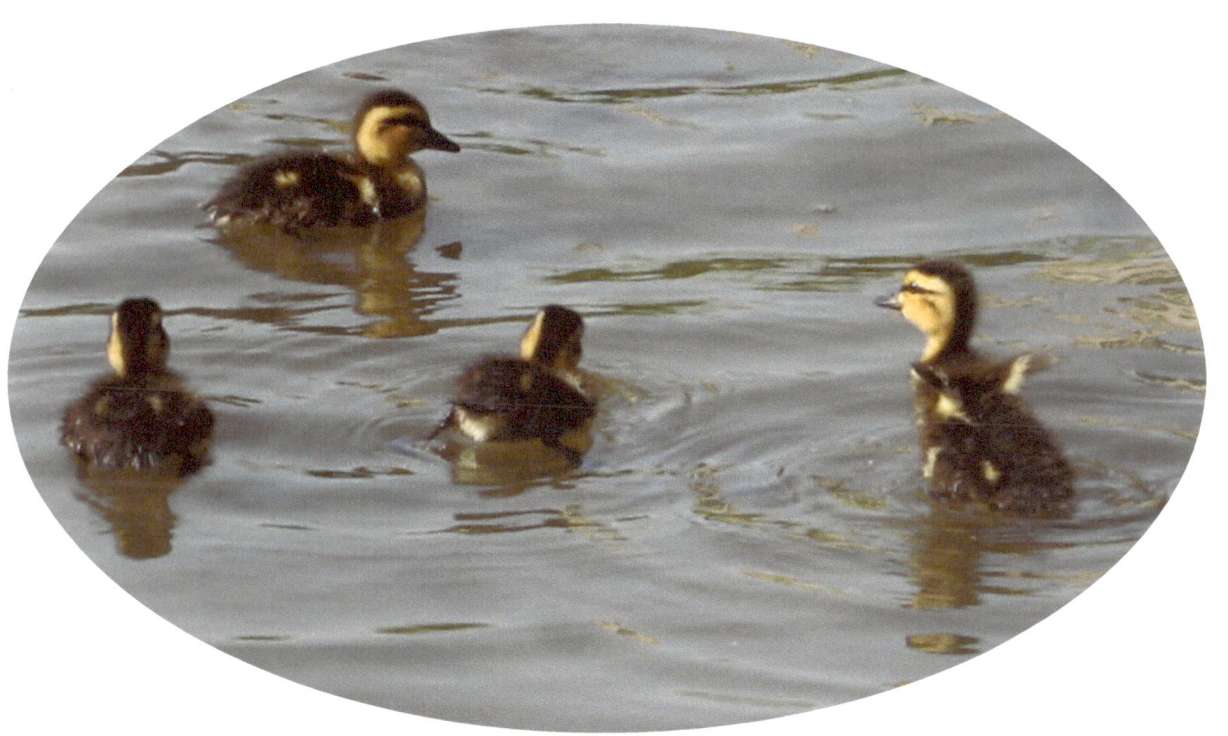

The Art of Nature

I AM KEEPING AN EYE ON EVERYONE

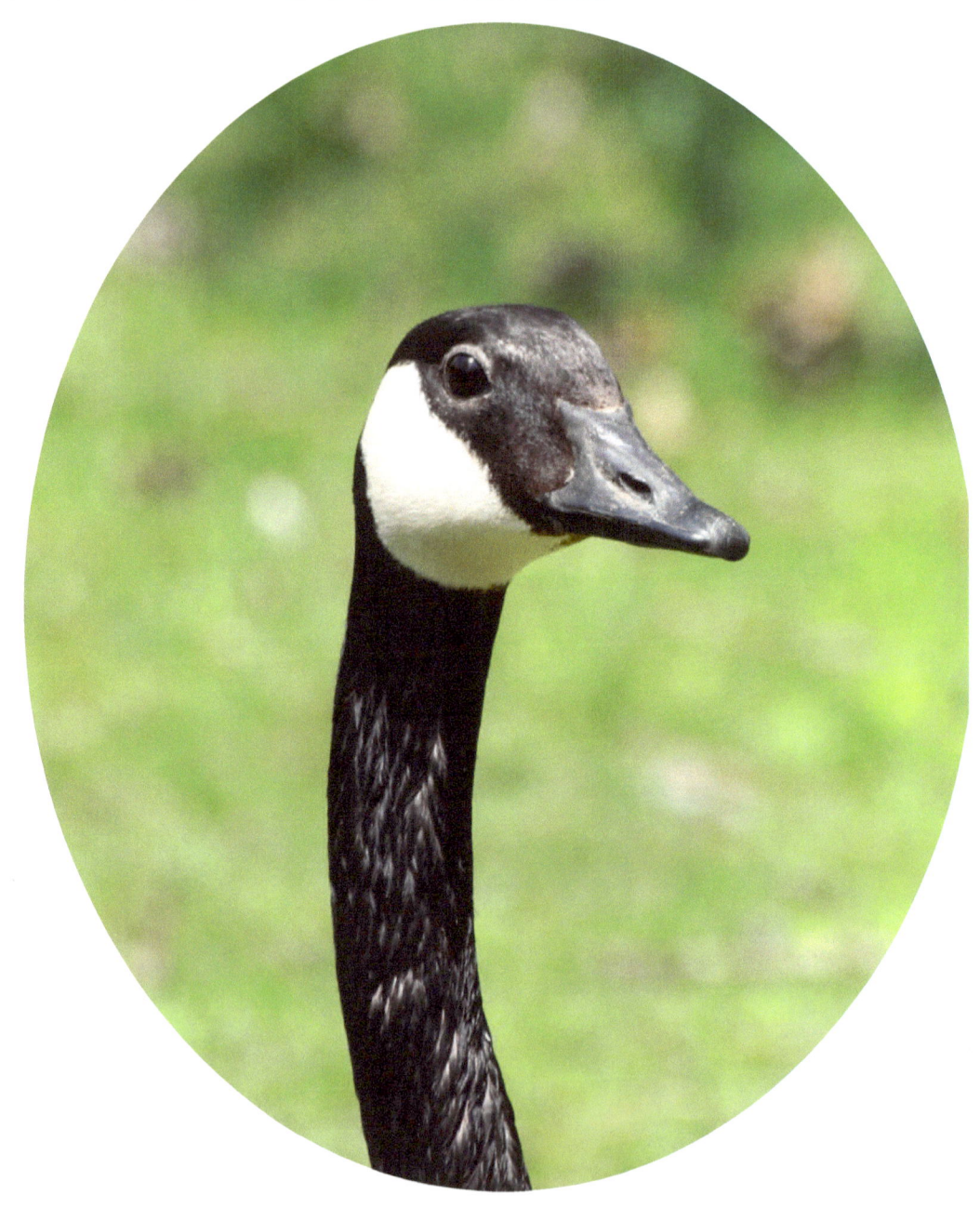

FLOWERS ARE THE JOY OF
HUMANITY

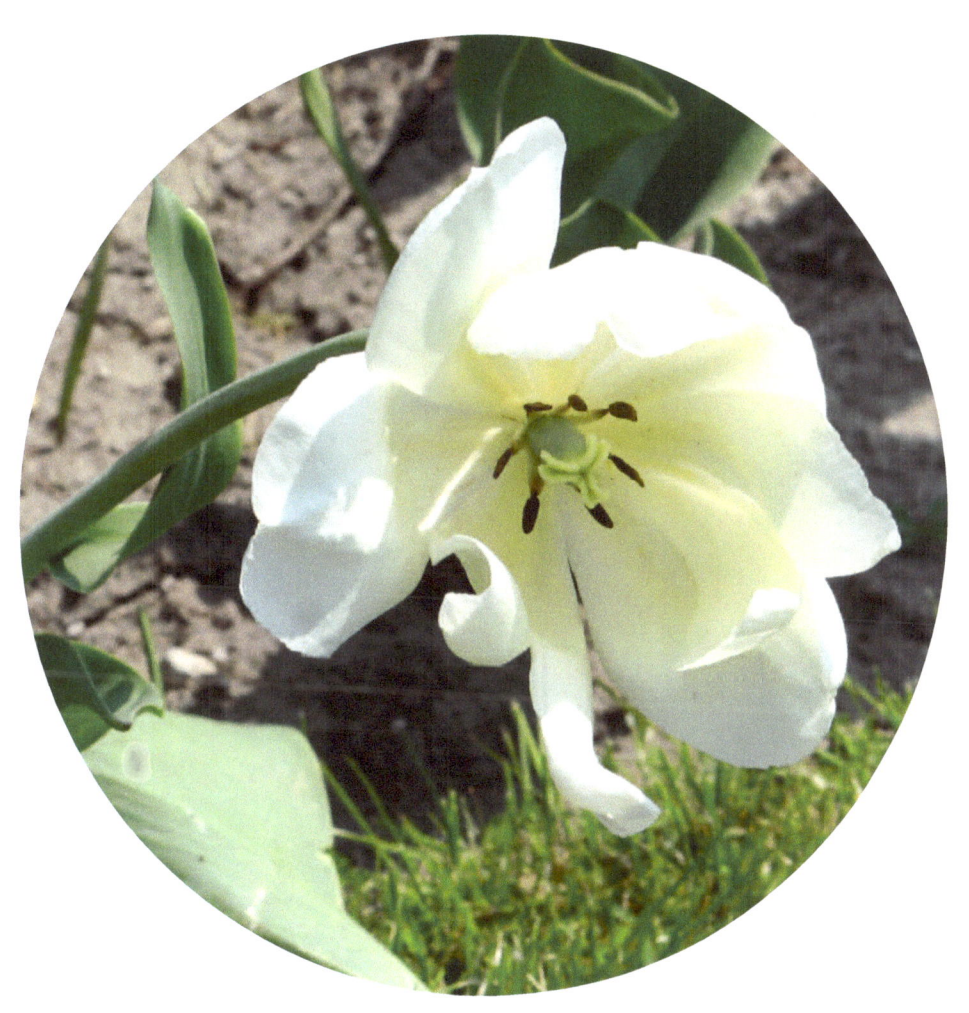

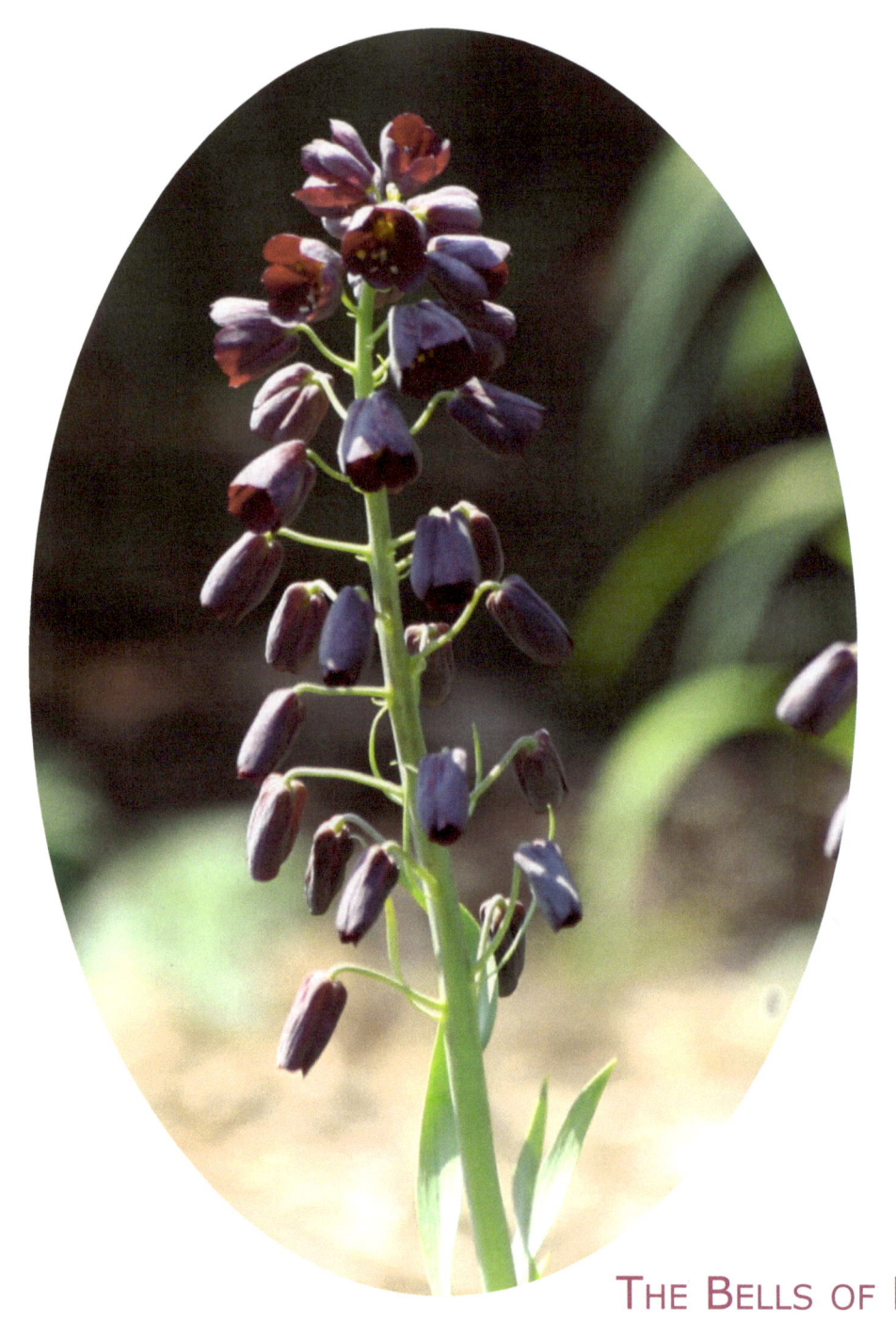

THE BELLS OF NATURE

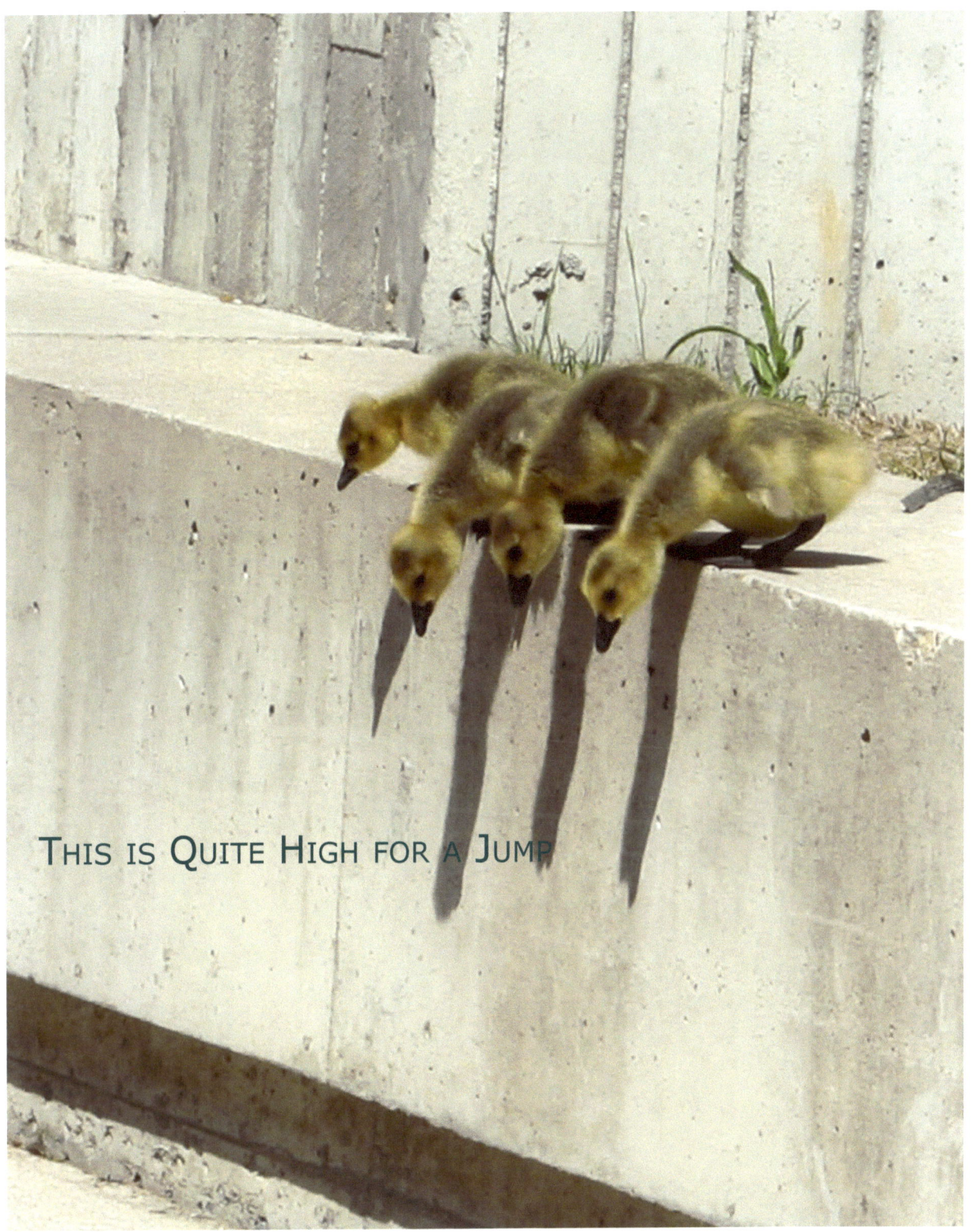

THIS IS QUITE HIGH FOR A JUMP

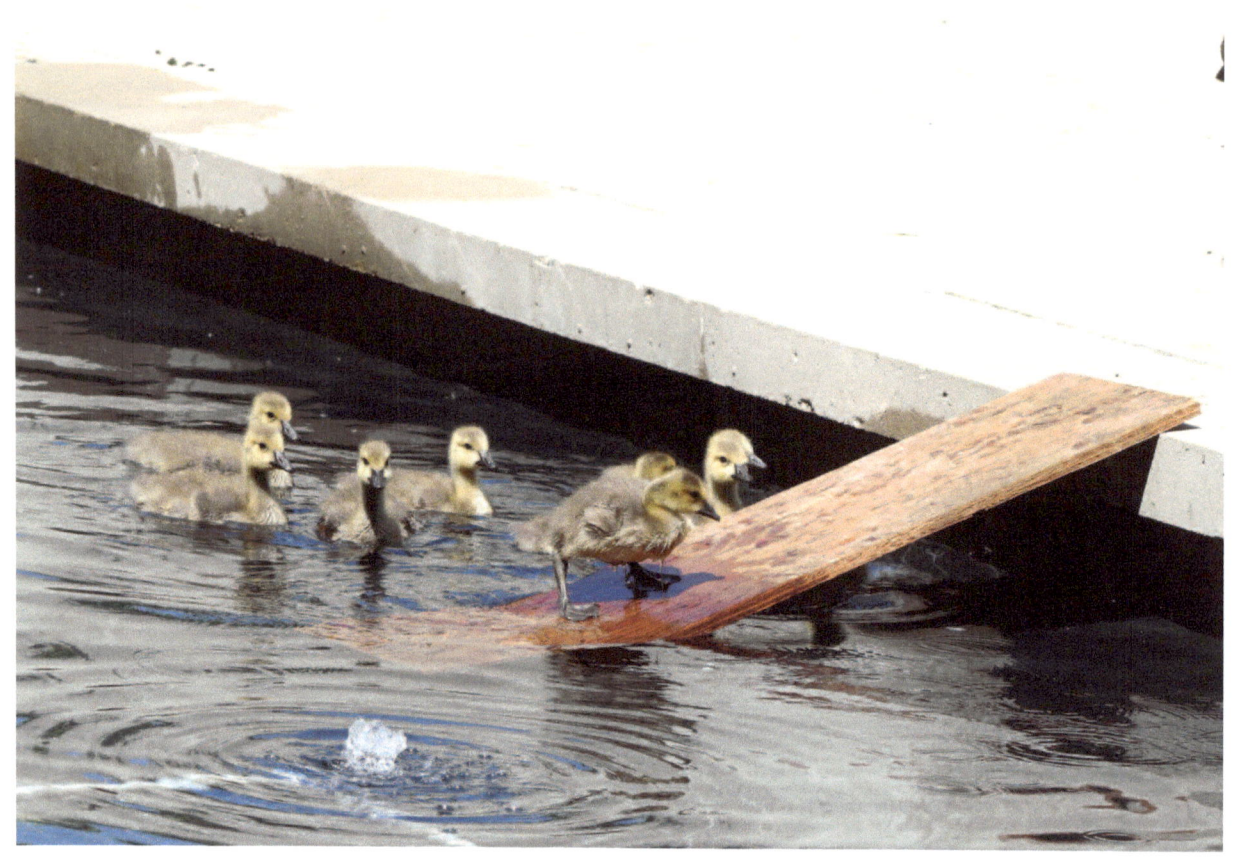

HURRAY! I FOUND A WAY OUT

The Art of Nature

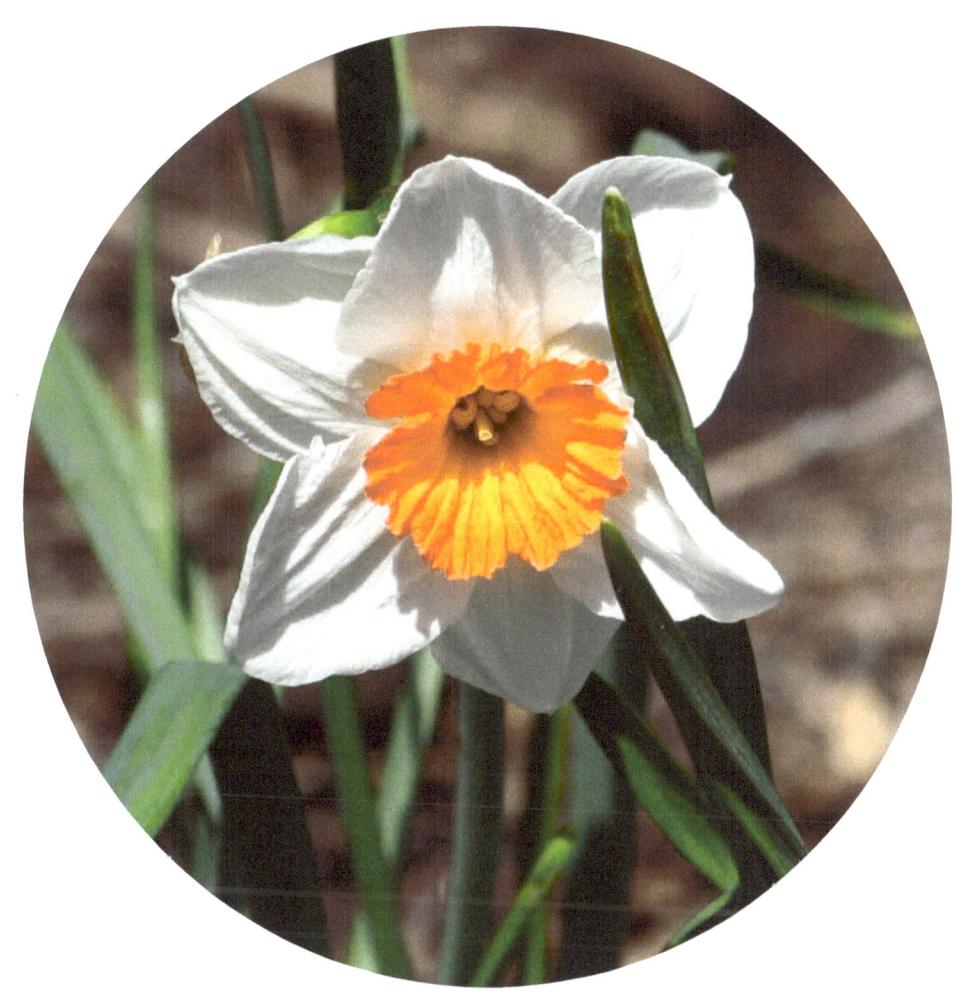

THE RICHNESS OF LIFE YOU WILL
FIND ONLY IN NATURE

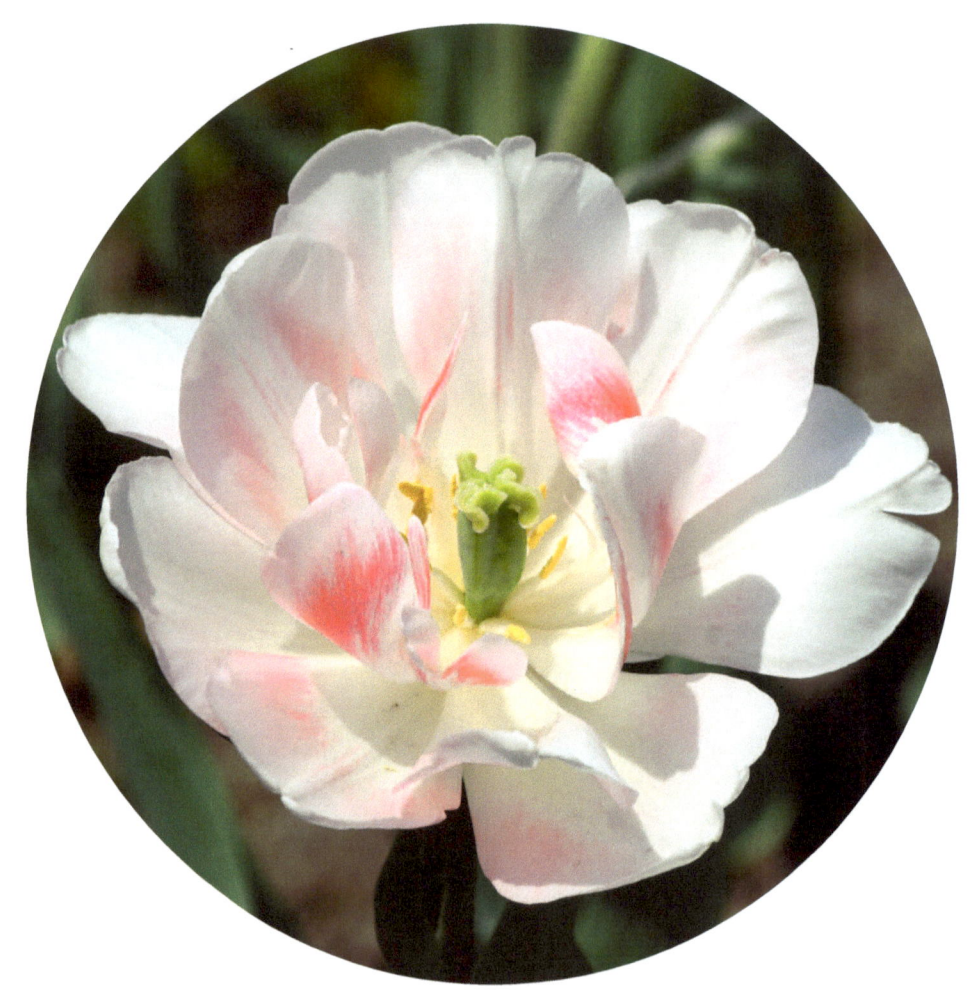

THIS FLOWER ... POETRY COMES
TO MIND

The Art of Nature

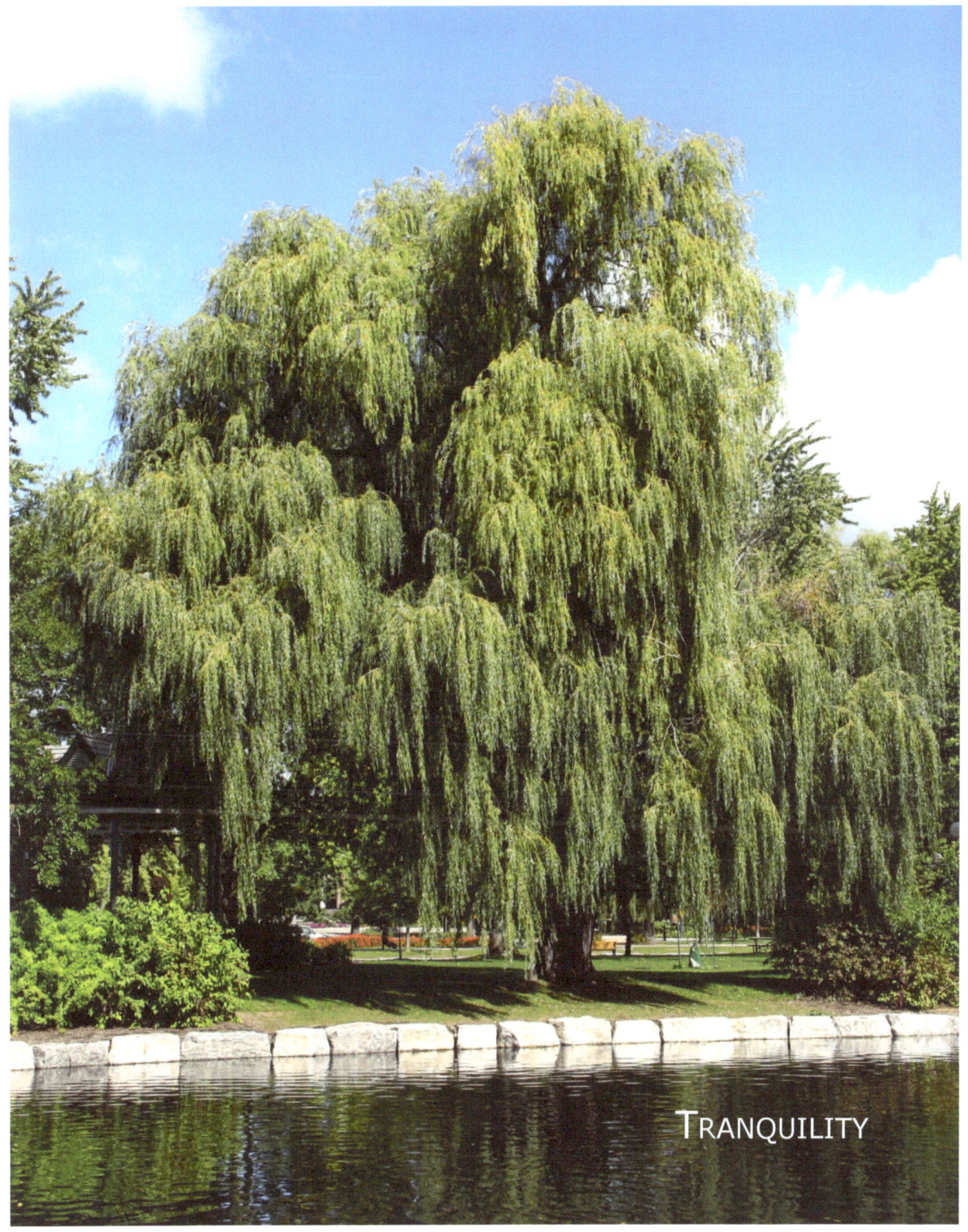

TRANQUILITY

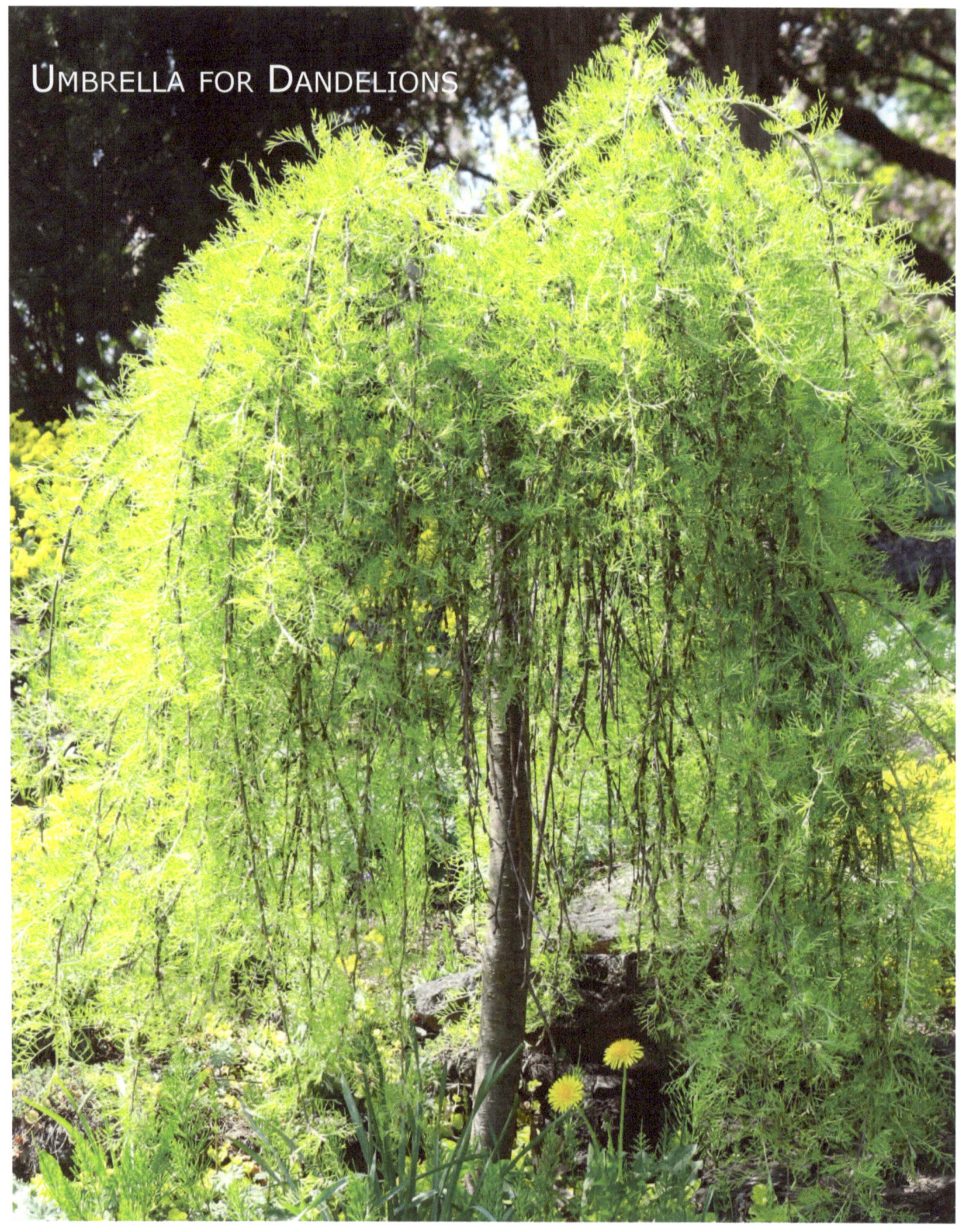

UMBRELLA FOR DANDELIONS

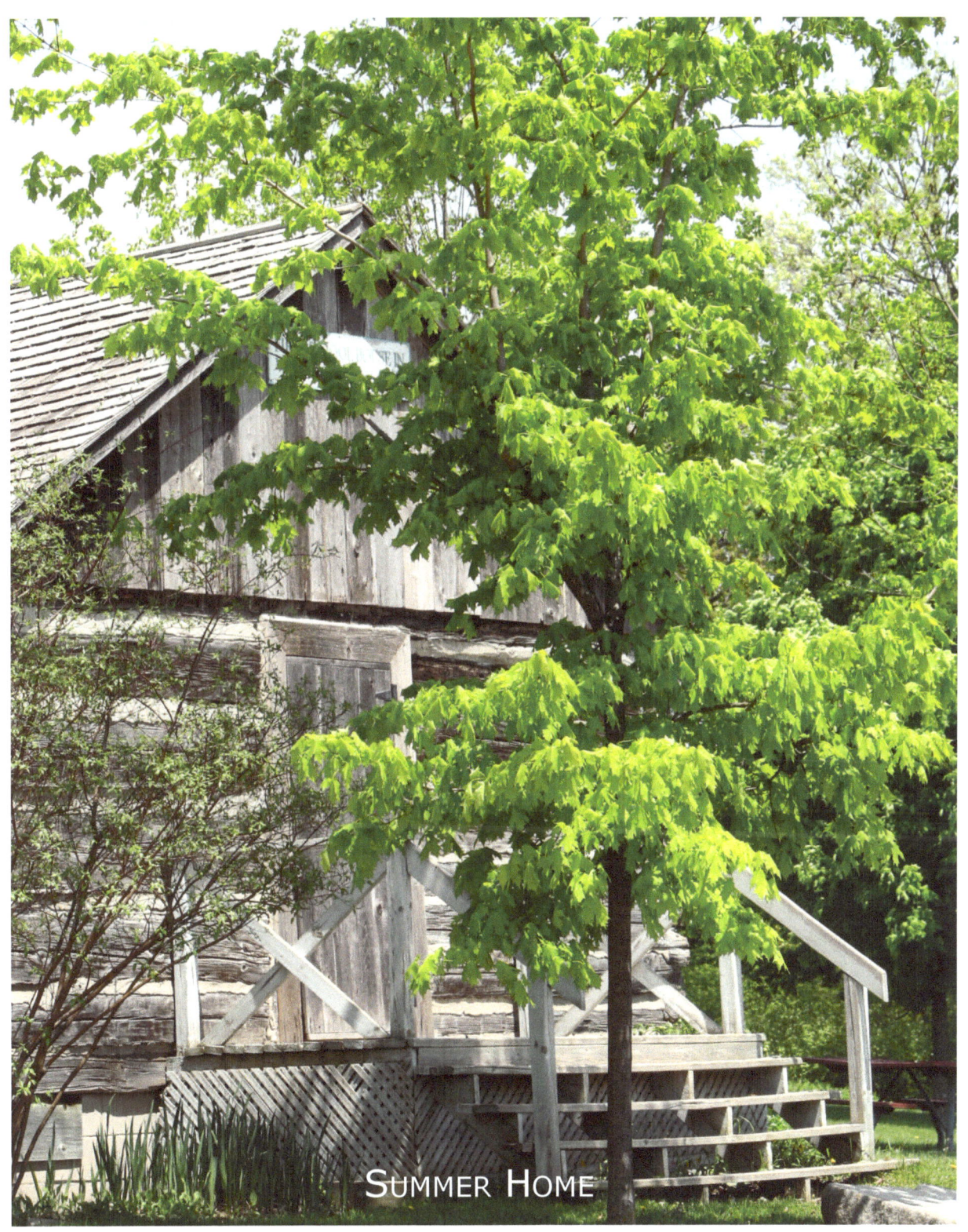

SUMMER HOME

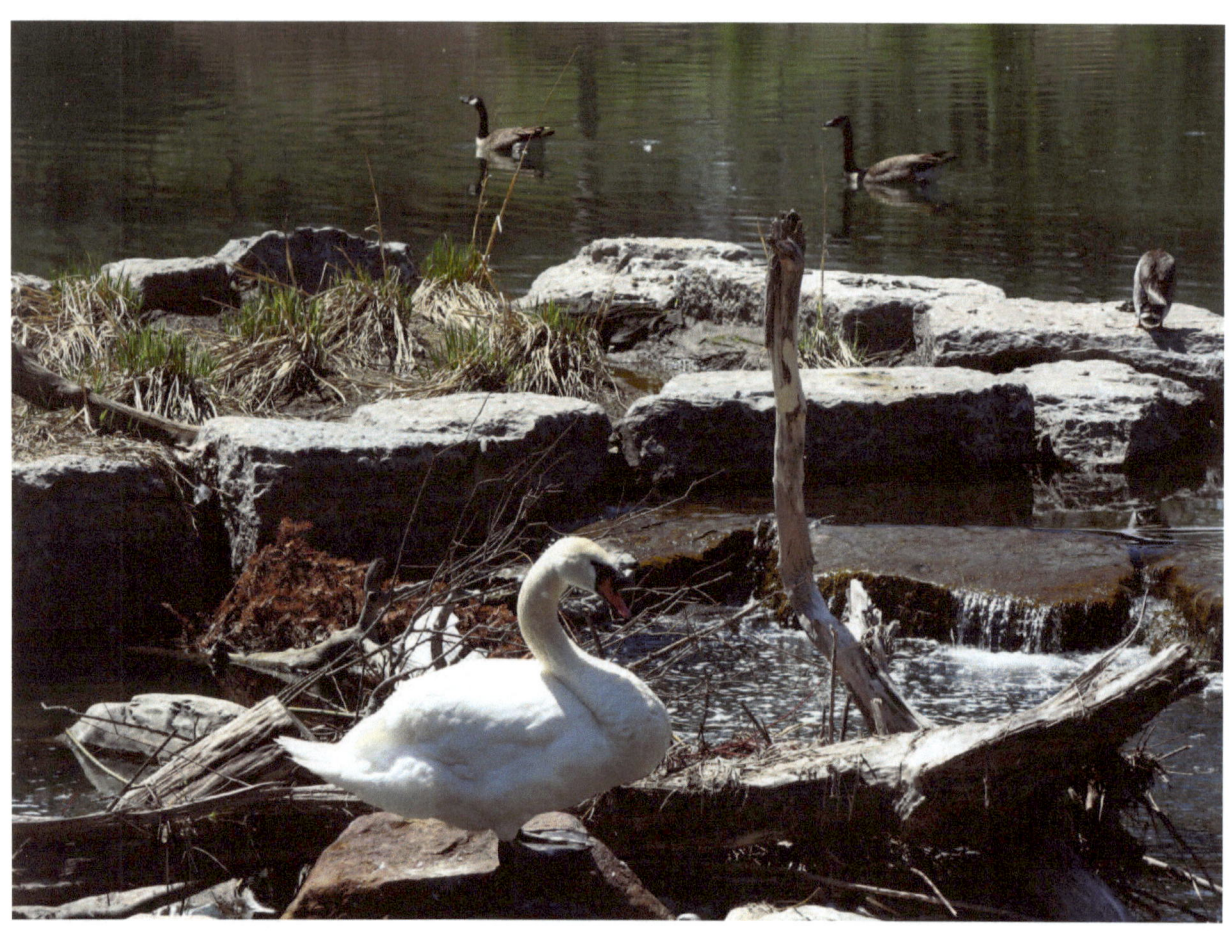

MY NEIGHBOURHOOD

PEEK A BOO

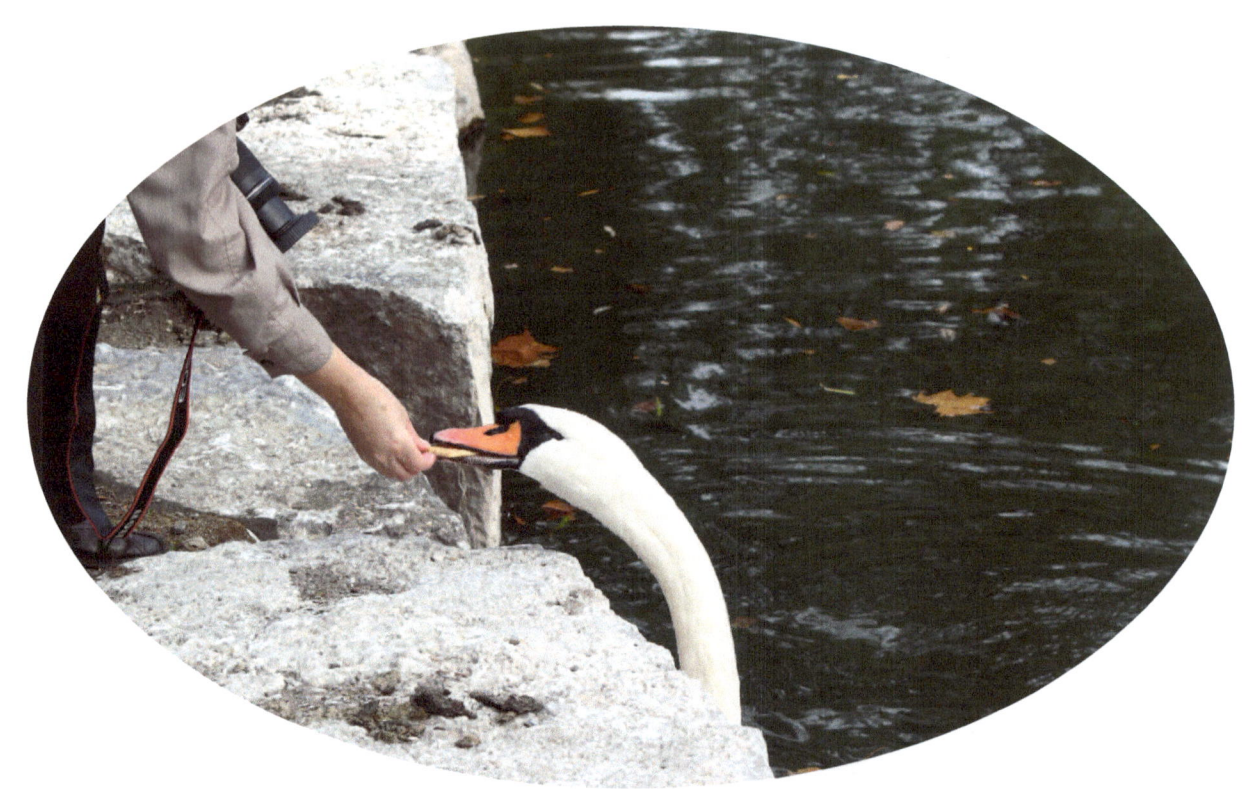

FINALLY A TEA BISCUIT

The Art of Nature

THE COLOURS OF FALL

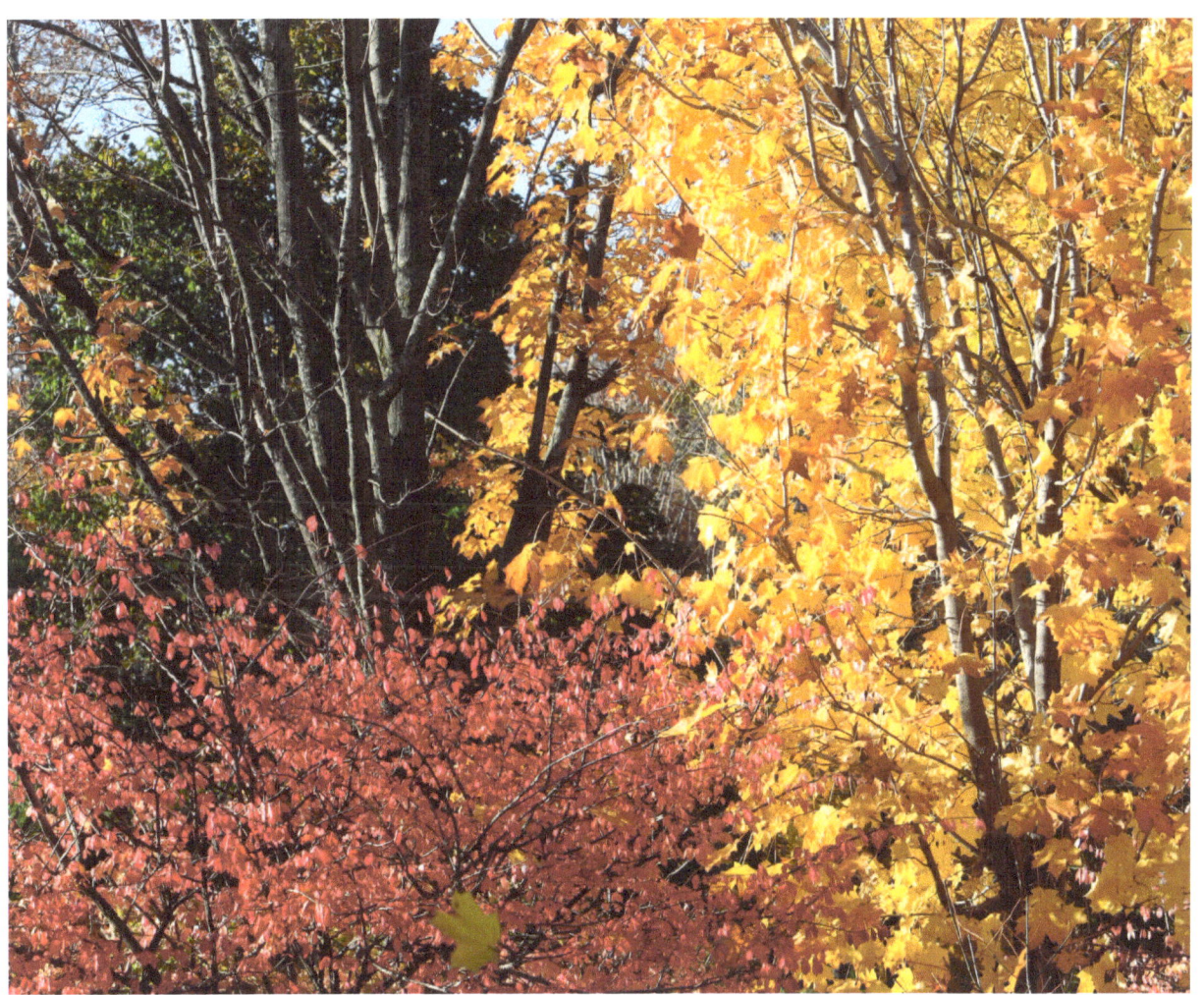

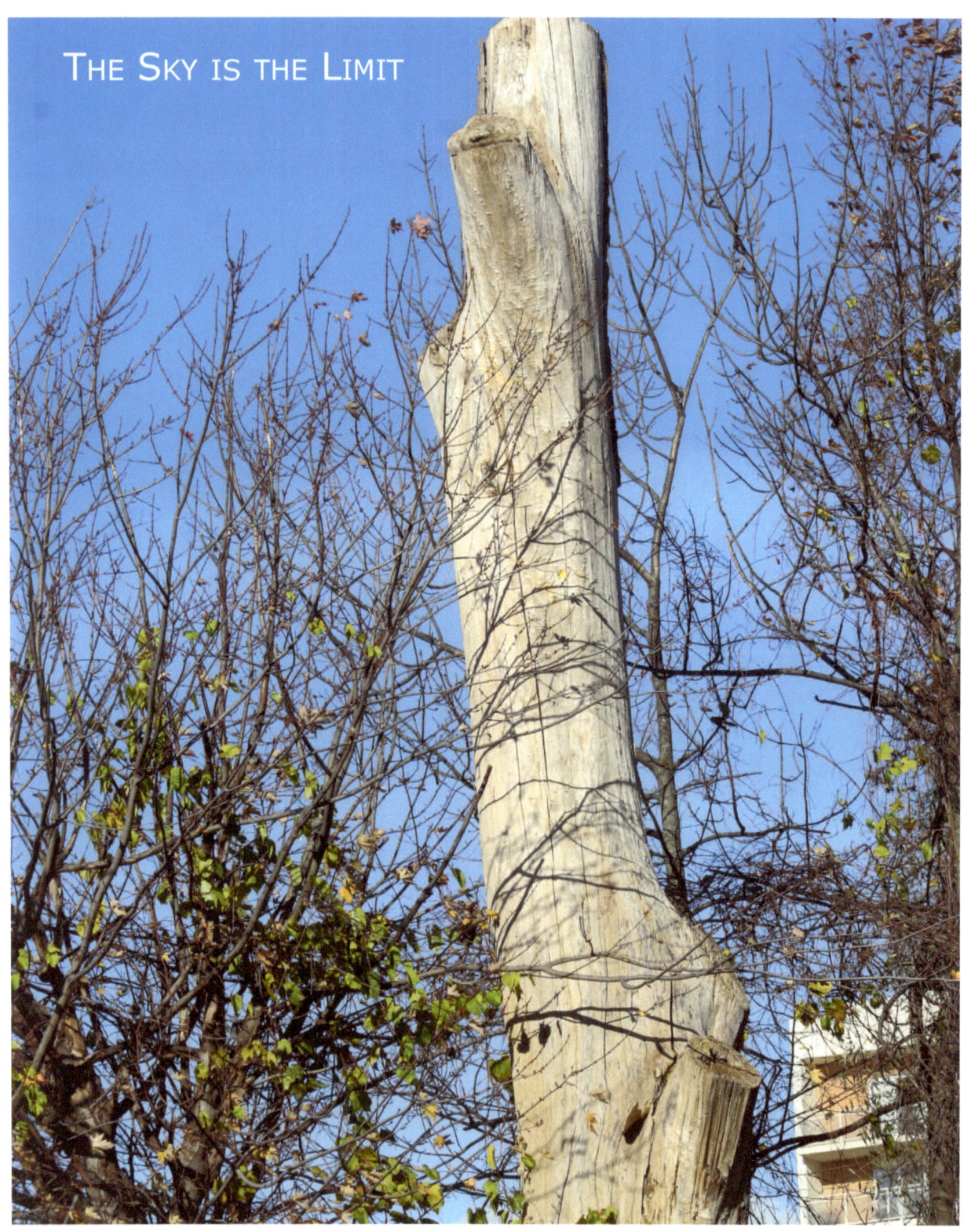

THE SKY IS THE LIMIT

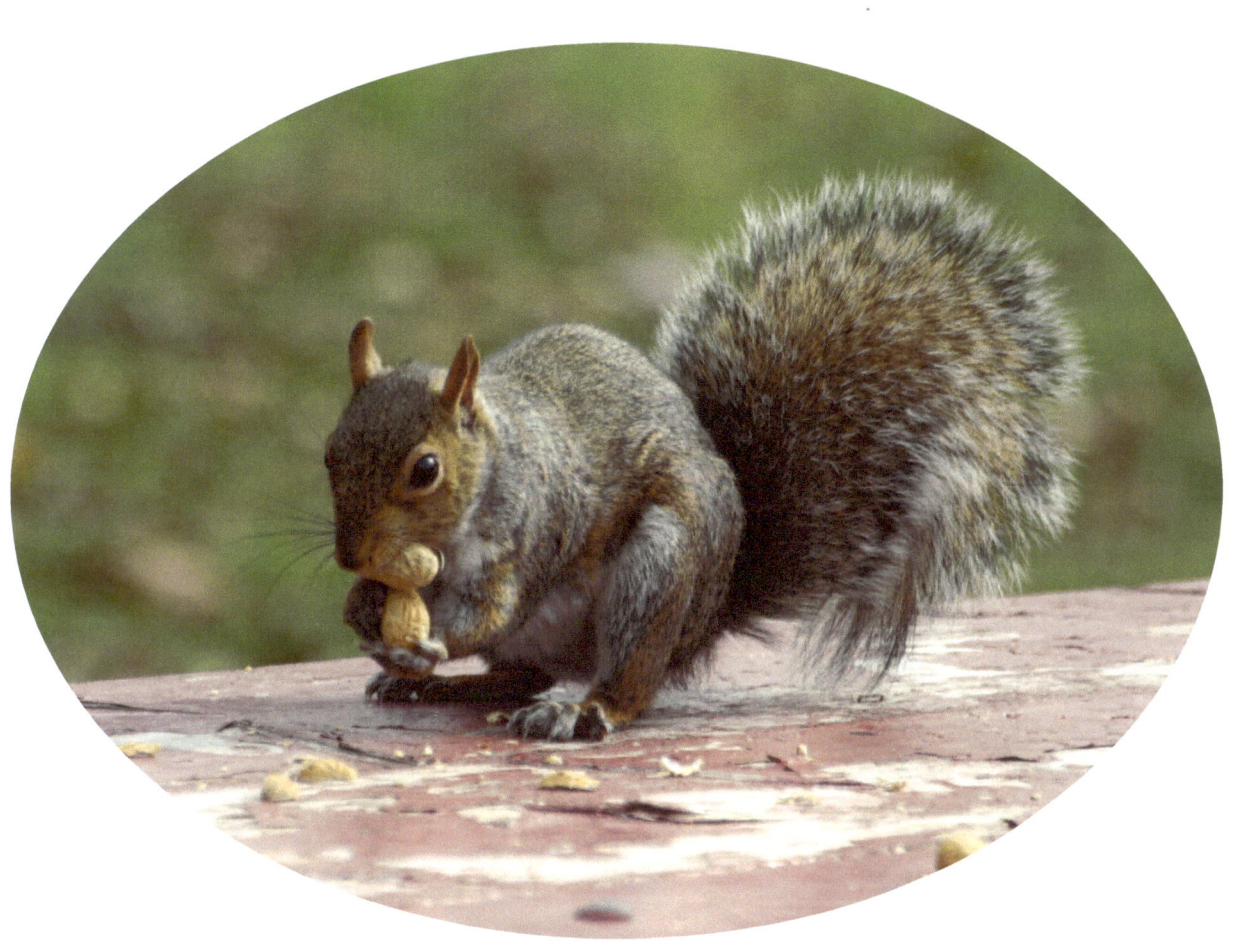

TIME TO STOCK UP! WINTER IS COMING

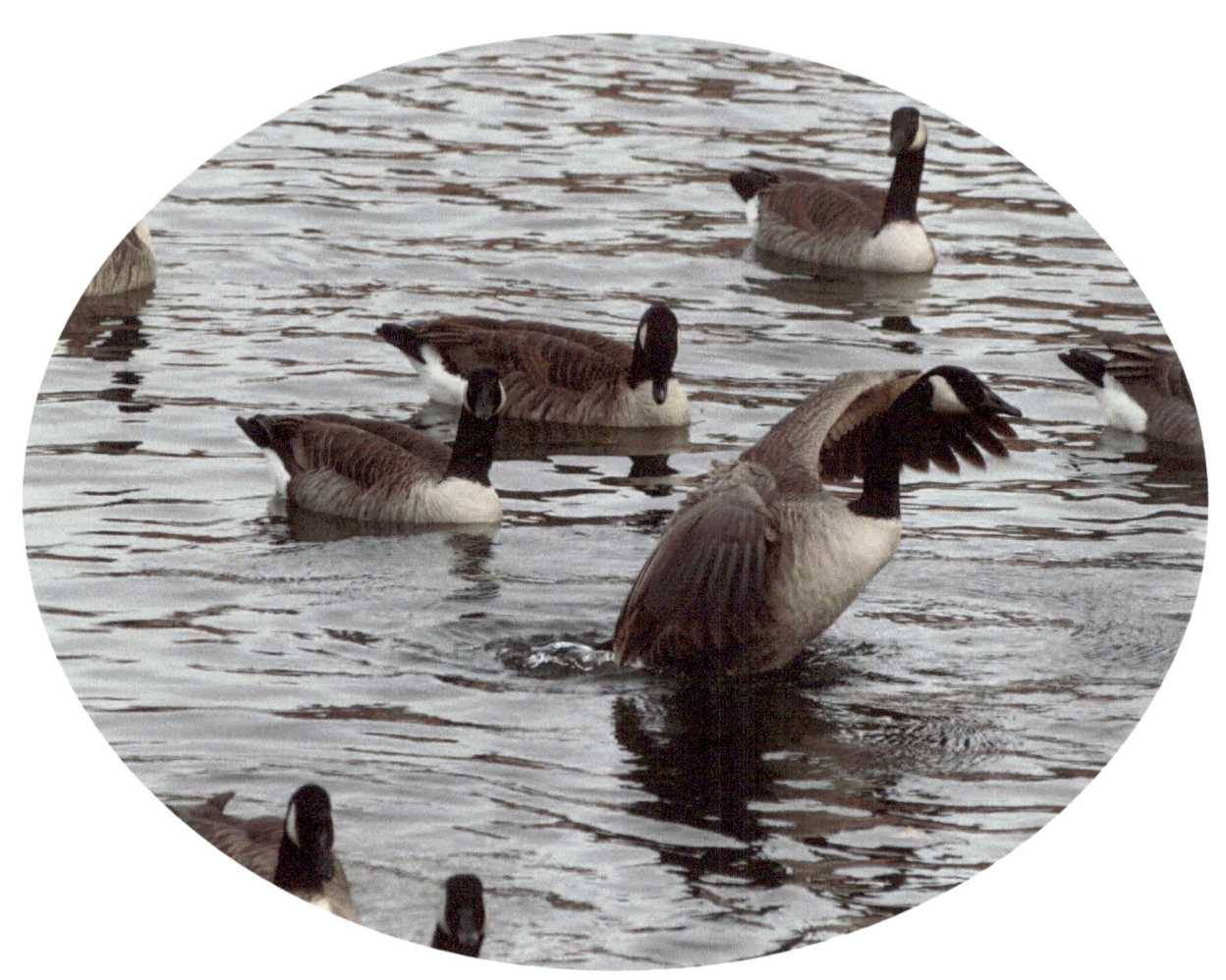

LADIES AND GENTLEMEN ...
TIME FOR ME TO TAKE OFF

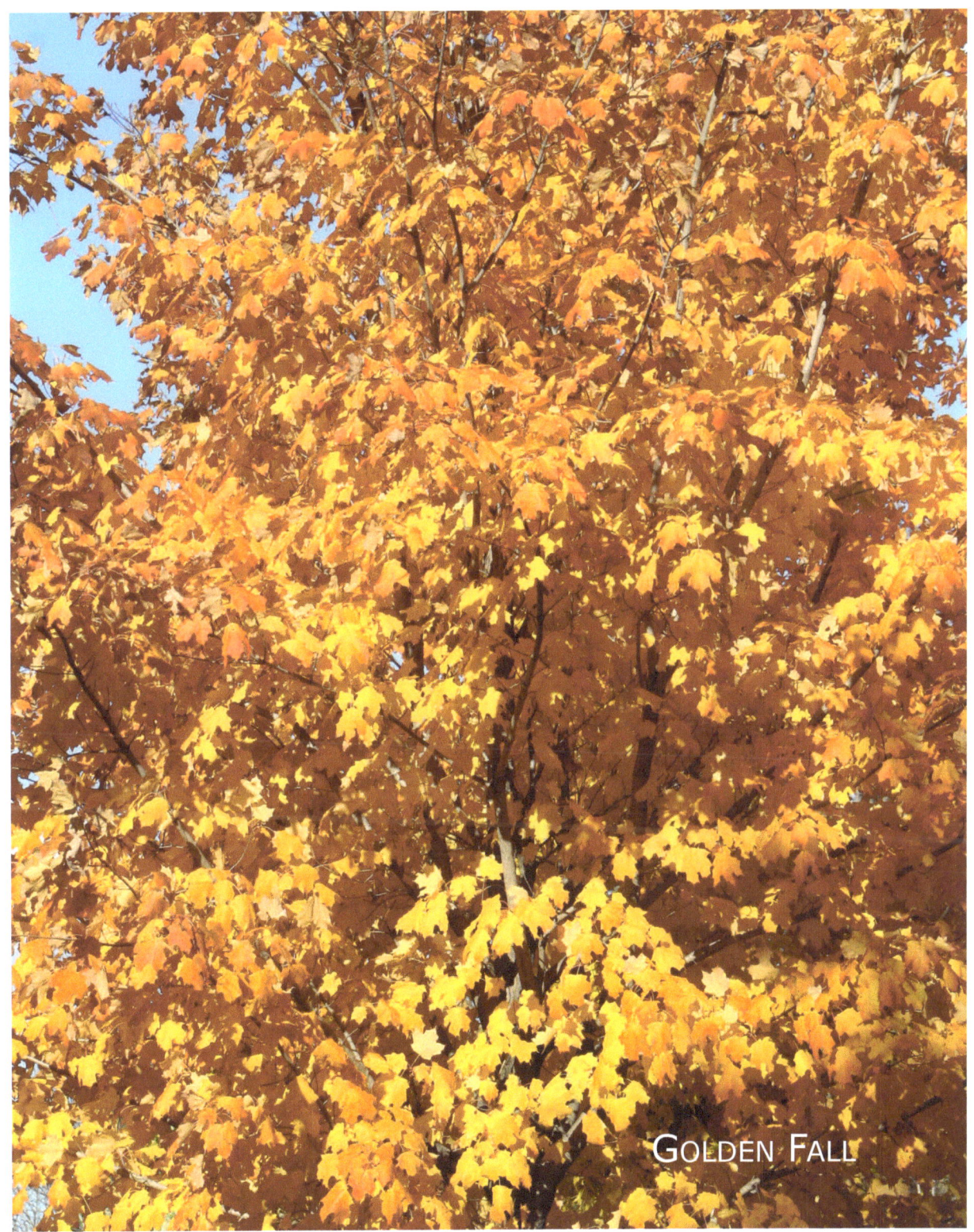

GOLDEN FALL

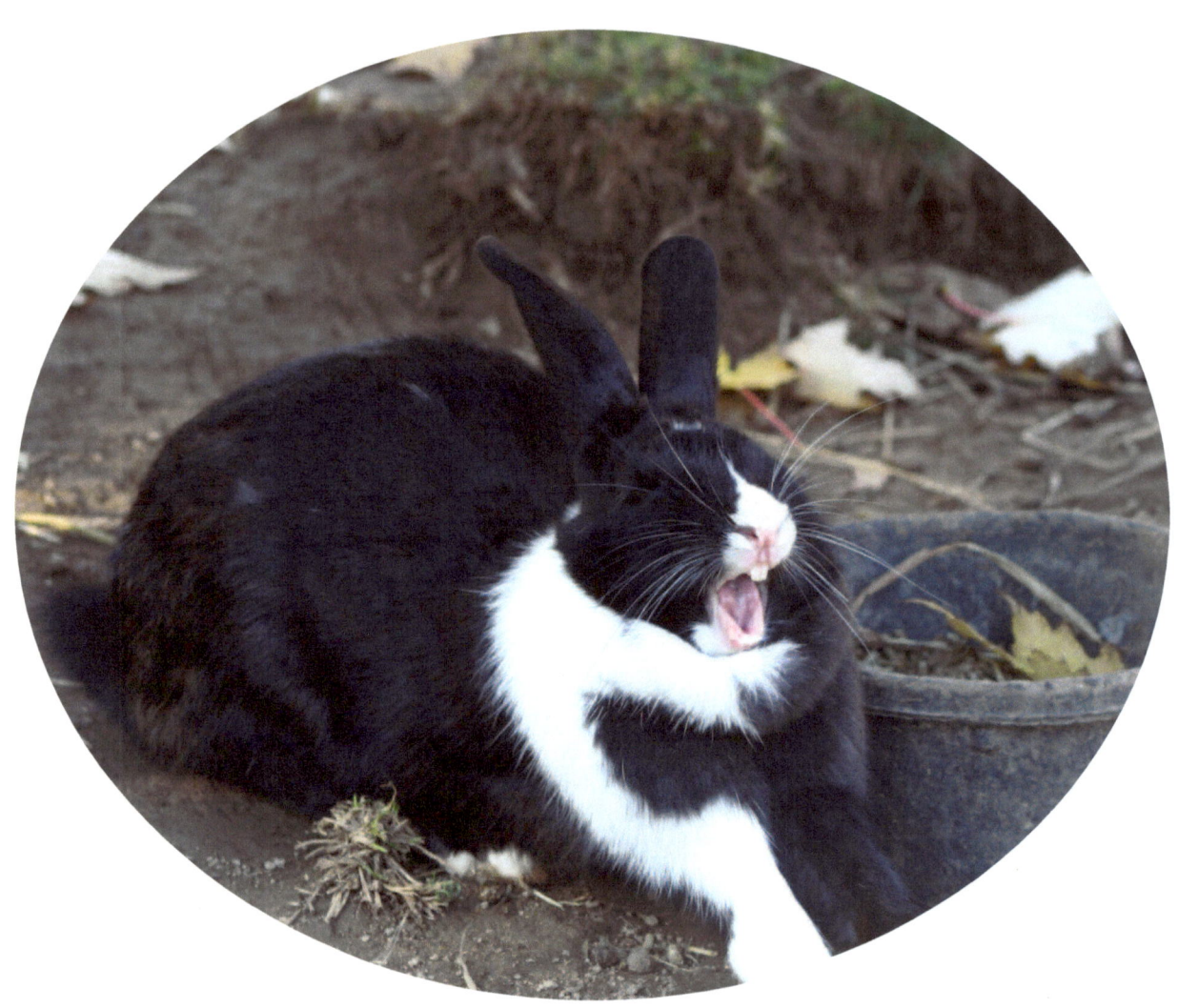

NOW IT IS HIGH TIME FOR
MY NAP

The Art of Nature

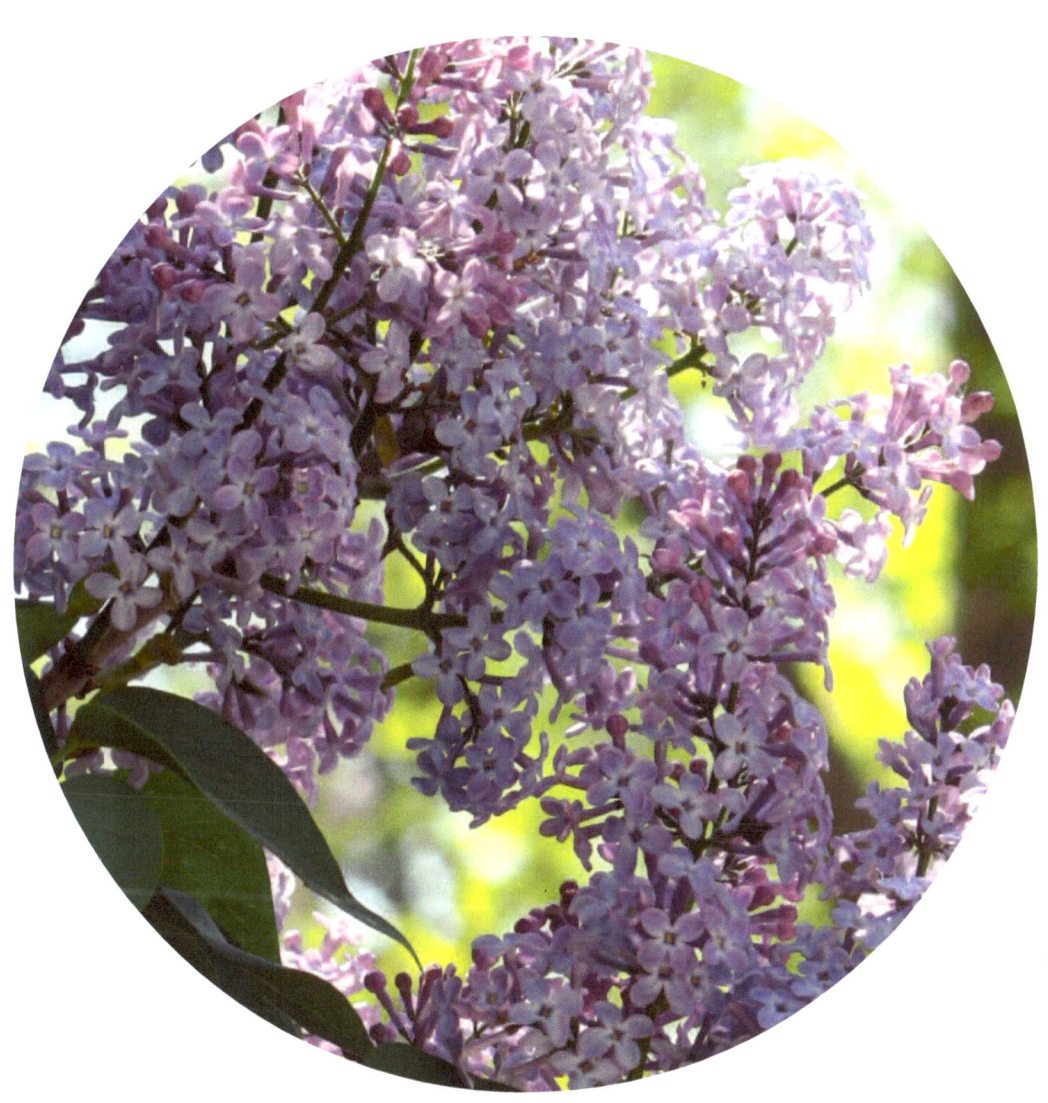

VIOLET DELIGHT

BIBLIOGRAPHY - KLAUS D. EMRICH

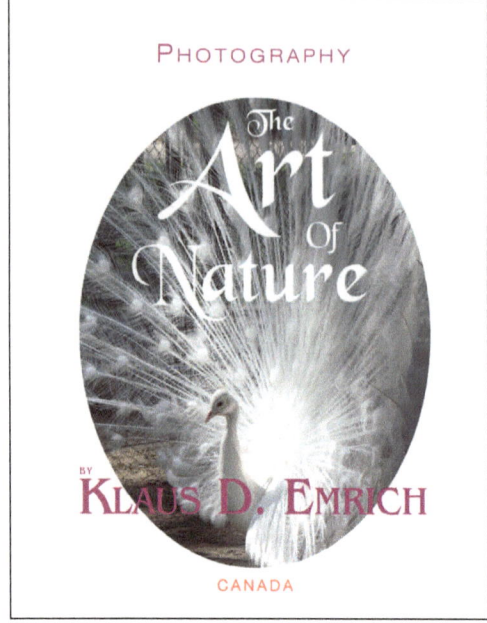

THE ART OF NATURE
Photography - Canadian nature.

BOOKS ALSO AVAILABLE IN GERMAN LANGUAGE.

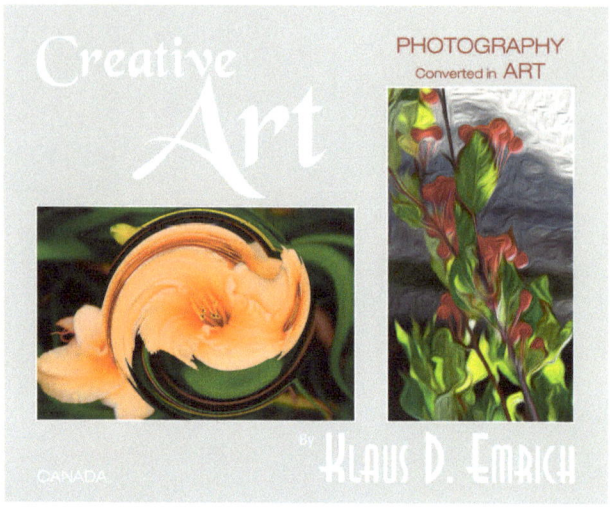

CREATIVE ART
Artistic view via photography.

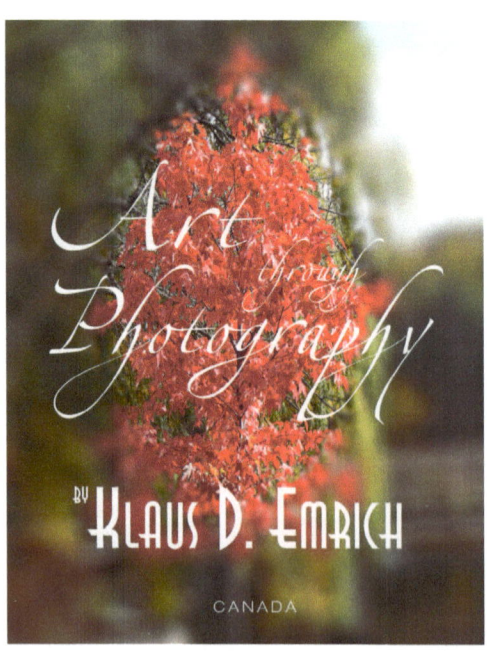

ART THROUGH PHOTOGRAPHY
Photography converted into art.

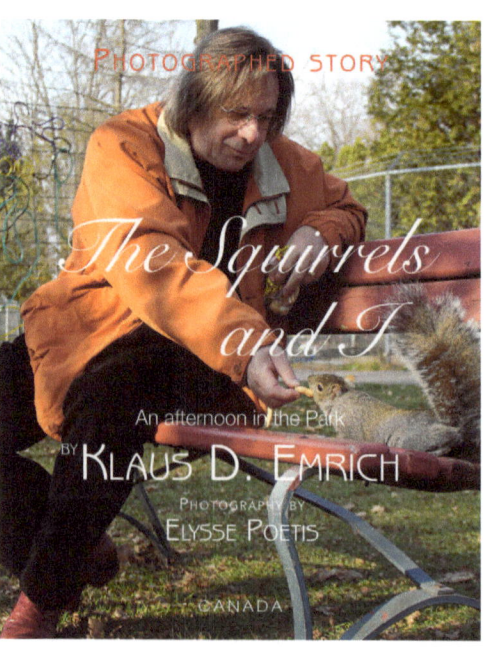

THE SQUIRRELS AND I
Photographed story.

ABOUT THE AUTHOR

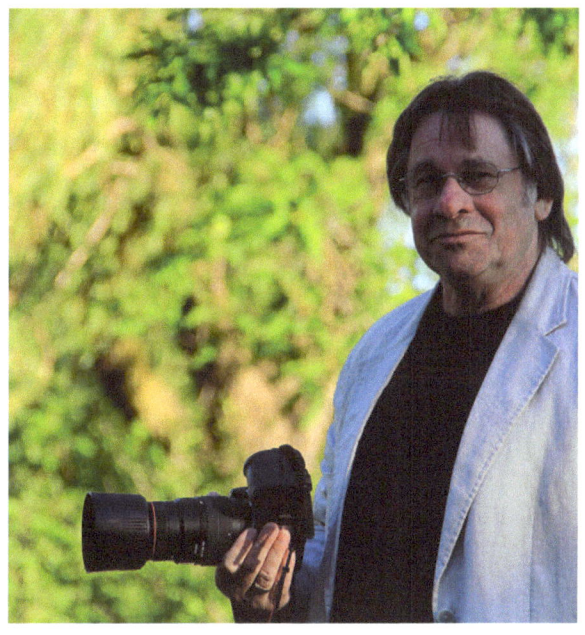

Klaus D. Emrich loved the art of nature since he was a small child back in Germany. He would go out in nature's fields and just stare at its beauty. Only in recent years did Klaus started using his talent/imagination via photography. Creating beauty was always his greatest dream. "The Art of Nature," published in 2014 by Von Der Alps Publishing Corporation, is Klaus' first book (with many more being prepared for publication).

Klaus D. Emrich and his wife Mary Emrich, (pseudonym Elysse Poetis, Award Winning author of many books on Amazon), reside in the famous Region of Waterloo, Ontario, CANADA.

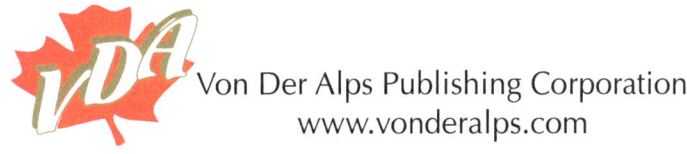
Von Der Alps Publishing Corporation
www.vonderalps.com

www.ingramcontent.com/pod-product-compliance
Lightning Source LLC
Chambersburg PA
CBHW040751200526
45159CB00025B/1844